D1329565

Bright Splinters of the Mind

Bright Splinters of the Mind

A personal story of research with autistic savants

Beate Hermelin

Foreword by Sir Michael Rutter

TOURO COLLEGE LIBRARY
Main Campus Midtown

WITHDRAWN

Jessica Kingsley Publishers
London and Philadelphia

M T

Some of the material in this book first appeared in the following journal articles: 'Native Savant Talent and Acquired Skill,' in *Autism 1*, 2, 1997, published by Sage Publications; 'Bottle, Tulip and Wineglass: Semantic and Structural Picture Processing by Savant Artists,' in *Journal of Child Psychology and Psychiatry 34*, 8, 1993, published by Pergamon Press; 'A Visually Impaired Savant Artist: Interacting Perceptual and Memory Representations,' in *Journal of Child Psychology and Psychiatry 40*, 7, 1999, published by Cambridge University Press; 'Visual Memory and Motor Programmes: Their Use by Idiot-Savant Artists and Controls,' in *British Journal of Psychology 78*, 1987, published by the British Psychological Society; 'Art and Accuracy: The Drawing Ability of Idiot-Savants,' in *Journal of Child Psychology and Psychiatry 31*, 2, 1990, published by Pergamon Press; 'The Recognition Failure and Graphic Success of Idiot-Savant Artists,' in *Journal of Clinical Psychology and Psychiatry 31*, 2, 1990, published by Pergamon Press; 'Visual and Graphic Abilities of the Idiot Savant Artist,' in *Psychological Medicine 17*, 1987, published by Cambridge University Press; 'A Savant Poet,' in *Psychological Medicine 26*, 1996, published by Cambridge University Press.

All rights reserved. No paragraph of this publication may be reproduced, copied or transmitted save with written permission or in accordance with the provisions of the Copyright Act 1956 (as amended), or under the terms of any licence permitting limited copying issued by the Copyright Licensing Agency, 33–34 Alfred Place, London WC1E 7DP. Any person who does any unauthorised act in relation to this publication may be liable to criminal prosecution and civil claims for damages.

The right of Beate Hermelin to be identified as author of this work has been asserted by her in accordance with the Copyright, Designs and Patents Act 1988.

First published in the United Kingdom in 2001 by
Jessica Kingsley Publishers Ltd
116 Pentonville Road
London N1 9JB, England
and
325 Chestnut Street
Philadelphia, PA 19106, USA

www.jkp.com

Copyright © 2001 Beate Hermelin
Foreword copyright © 2001 Sir Michael Rutter

Library of Congress Cataloging in Publication Data
A CIP catalog record for this book is available from the Library of Congress

British Library Cataloguing in Publication Data
A CIP catalogue record for this book is available from the British Library

ISBN 1 85302 932 7 pb
ISBN 1 85302 931 9 hb

Printed and Bound in Great Britain by
Athenaeum Press, Gateshead, Tyne and Wear

6/11/02

Contents

List of Plates

List of Figures

In Remembrance of Neil O'Connor

Acknowledgements

I would like to express my gratitude to the Trustees of The Nuffield Foundation. Without their generous support much of the research reported here could not have been carried out, and this book would not have been written.

I would also like to thank my collaborators with whom I was privileged to work, and my friends and colleagues for their constructive comments while writing this book.

The illustrations were initially published in the following journals: *Psychological Medicine*, *Autism*, *British Journal of Psychology* and *Journal of Child Psychology and Psychiatry*.

Foreword

In the course of my work as a scientist and as a clinician I have to read an immense number of books. Many are wonderfully interesting and informative, and some (rather fewer) are a pleasure to read because their style is so lively and creative in conveying enthusiasm and conceptual clarity. It is very much rarer to come across books that have all these high qualities but, in addition, present an exciting voyage of discovery which leads to a new integration of ideas, and succeed in making what hitherto appeared complicated and unknowable seem simple and understandable. This book is one of those rarities. It tells a compelling story that makes the book very difficult to put down. But much more, although not written for that purpose, it shows vividly and grippingly something of the key qualities that have made Beate Hermelin one of the most brilliantly innovative experimental psychologists of the day, as well as one of the most engaging individuals. She portrays her goal as giving readers an understanding of the mental strategies that underlie the extraordinary talents shown by so-called idiots savant, most of whom are autistic. She achieves that objective in splendid fashion but, in doing so, she accomplishes the more difficult feat of conveying both why science is so exciting, and how scientists tackle the task of testing hypotheses that pit one explanation against others. The general public sometimes thinks of science as providing factual information but, actually, that is not what science is about at all. Of course it gives rise to 'facts' and it has to make use of those 'facts', but its purpose is to find out what they *mean* – the *how* rather than the *what*.

For the scientists, savant talents constitute a challenge. How can individuals who are so impaired in their general mental functioning that they need to be looked after by others, nevertheless show specific skills in one domain that are spectacularly better than those possessed by most individuals of high intelligence? What do the answers tell us about mental functioning generally and what light is thrown on the nature of the disorder, autism, that constitutes this background? For humanists, the talents provide a source of wonder and awe with regard to a most remarkable and seemingly mysterious phenomenon. For specialists in the areas for which the talents are shown, the skills raise questions on the very basis of their speciality. Do the talents of a musical savant have anything in common with the creative precocity of, say, Mozart? Have the spectacular drawing skills of artistic savants any connections with creative painting? What have calendar savants' talents got to do with 'real' mathematics? One of the very special qualities of this remarkable book is that, not only are all three perspectives brought together, but it is made clear that they *have* to be combined if scientific enquiry is truly to succeed in its objectives. Throughout the book, Beate Hermelin shows respect for the individuals whose savant skills she studied. Doubtless, that played an important role in her great success in gaining their cooperation for the experimental studies but, also, it shows that rigorous searching scientific enquiry can be combined with a compassionate concern and appreciation of the individuality of the people whose qualities are being studied in such incisive, dispassionate fashion.

In that spirit, each chapter on a particular talent begins with a mini-lesson on some of the key qualities involved in that skill domain — be it music, art, mathematics, or the construction of calendars. These are gems in themselves, blending science, literature and history in a wonderfully engaging, easy to read fashion. But this is light years away from ivory tower academia. The crucial underlying point is that, if the savant skill is to be investigated, it is necessary first to understand what is involved in the 'ordinary' skill at its highest levels. Accordingly, the research undertaken involved collaboration with mathematicians, musicians and artists. Readers will, along the way to understanding savant skills, come to appreciate much more about these areas of creativity.

But let me turn to the science, for that constitutes the heart of the book. How were the experiments formulated? What were they trying to do? How did they determine which explanation was more likely to be correct? The reader will look in vain for the usual paraphernalia of science – samples, measures and statistics – but they will learn how these were used to test competing hypotheses. In all cases, the research strategy involved three key components. First, the patterns of successes and failures shown by the savants were compared with those shown by experts in the skill domain and by 'ordinary' people from the general population. Second, the successes and failures of the savants were compared (within themselves) according to ingenious variations in both the nature of the tasks and the ways in which the tasks were presented. Third, in devising both of these comparisons, the researchers used their knowledge of the skill areas to devise tasks that relied on a particular way of solving the problem or which tested the effects of practice or of some other skill.

For example, in studying an individual who had a command of multiple foreign languages, it was shown that his skills applied to the elements of language as provided by words, morphemes (the smallest divisible parts of words), and prefixes/suffixes, rather than by grammar. The savant showed a remarkable facility in many aspects of reading and translating multiple languages, but could not focus on the meaning of sentences as a whole and did not show the same facility to acquire new grammatical rules. Similarly, by focusing on calendrical and dating tests that could and could not use the rule that the structure of the year repeats itself every 28 years, or which focused on non-rule-based datings (such as Easter), it was shown that the savants used rule-based strategies and not just rote memory. The skills of autistic savants were found not to rely on a particular ability in remembering visual patterns; they made normal use of pictorial rules and perspectives and were well able to adapt someone else's visual perspective even though they could not adopt (or even appreciate) their mind set. Musical savants could generate music as well as reproduce it but, again, they followed rule structures.

By making comparisons across these skill domains, as well as across tasks within each domain, Beate Hermelin concludes that the unifying feature is that the savants use the strategy of taking a mental path from single units to a subsequent higher order extraction of overarching patterns and structures. This is the opposite of what most people do in their thinking and in their mental task performance. That is to say, we use our appreciation of meaning, and of the gestalt whole, to come up with answers on the specifics. For the most part, we are not very good at solving problems in the abstract when we cannot use meaning and familiarity to help us. That does not seem to apply to savants with respect to their specific talents, but the skills are mostly remarkably circumscribed. They do not reassess, redo and reorganise their creative output and, because of that, their exceptional productions tend to give the impression of a first draft rather than a final production. Their ways of doing things make them very much better than other people in some respects but more constrained in others. We need to understand (as well as admire) the reasons for their incredible accomplishments but, equally, we need to appreciate why these do not lead on to artistic or scientific innovations.

In a striking fashion, Beate Hermelin shows how these goals require experiments that give rise to *both* successes and failures. We learn very little from failures on their own because there are so many reasons for not being able to perform a task. The skill of creative scientists lies in devising experiments in which the set-up predicts success if one explanation is correct but failure if another provides the answer. The book has a beautiful lightness of touch in exemplifying how this approach was used to study savant skills.

Read on to understand the science, but also read on to appreciate the excitement of being a scientist involved in making discoveries. Beate Hermelin is realistic about how much more is needed to provide a full understanding, but her work, as in her broader set of studies of autism, has opened up new territories in ways that force us to rethink our ideas on some of the basic concepts. The book, incidentally, also shows what a special talent Beate Hermelin has for writing about science for a broader audience. But this book is a 'must' for scientists as well as for the general public, because of the clarity of its expression of an experimental approach to special abilities and disabilities.

Sir Michael Rutter
November 2000

1

Outline

In 1850 Alfred, Lord Tennyson wrote a poem which he dedicated to the memory of a very talented man, who overcame the worst circumstances of his 'lowly birth'. Tennyson wrote that he who is gifted is someone:

Who breaks his birth's invidious bar,
And grasps the skirts of happy chance,
And breasts the blows of circumstance,
And grapples with his evil star.

This verse could just as well refer to an 'idiot savant', a term used to describe a person who, despite being mentally handicapped and usually also autistic, nevertheless possesses an outstanding ability in a specific domain such as art, music or arithmetic. In the past, people who could not cope with the complexities of life were classified as being either 'idiots', 'imbeciles' or 'feeble minded', according to the degree of severity of their mental impairment. In Britain these labels were abolished in 1959 following a Royal Commission report in 1957 on 'The Law as it Relates to Mental Illness and Mental Deficiency'. The Commission's report defined 'mental deficiency' as applying to 'those persons whose general personality is so severely subnormal, that the patient is incapable of living an independent life'.

Mental deficiency, as it was then called, is not in itself a disease nor is it a single entity. Although a diminished capacity for reasoning and learning is shared generally by those so diagnosed, this is due to a multitude of different causes. These can be a consequence of genetic factors, prenatal or birth trauma, or later illnesses and accidents which effect the efficiency of brain functioning. Impaired mental processes may also be due to as yet less well-defined causes, as for instance is the case with autism.

Mental impairment as a consequence of such varying factors had been recognised for a long time, and its characteristics were set out in a classic account by Treadgold in 1909. However, its systematic scientific investigation by psychologists only took off in the early 1950s, and in Britain it was pioneered by the Medical Research Council's Jack Tizard and Neil O'Connor as well as by the clinical psychologists Ann and Alan Clarke. I joined the MRC in 1956, when O'Connor and I began our long research collaboration, aimed at introducing experimental methods into studies focusing on the language and thinking of mentally handicapped and autistic children. In the course of these investigations we had to travel all over the country to see these young people in their institutions, special residential schools and sheltered communities. During these visits it occasionally happened that we came across someone who, in spite of general mental handicap, appeared to possess a quite outstanding special ability.

We knew of course that accounts of 'idiots savants' had been given for over 100 years. The Frenchman Alfred Binet, who invented the first intelligence test, had introduced the term to describe those people who had great learning difficulties and could not cope with life on their own, but yet showed an outstanding ability in a specific area. In fact, as only those with the very lowest intelligence levels fell into the category of 'idiots', the term 'idiot savant' was probably never quite appropriate. Now it is estimated that about half of such individuals, especially those with autism, obtain scores on at least one or more sub-tests of general intelligence that put them into the range of normal functioning. However, it remains true that because of their mental impairments savants usually cannot live independently and need constant help and support.

A savant is a rare phenomenon. Between 2 and 3 per cent of the population suffer from some degree of mental handicap, but only 0.06 per cent of these had initially been estimated to possess an unusually high level of specific ability that is far above that of the average normal person. As I will discuss in more detail later on, it is noteworthy that savant ability is much more frequently found in those who suffer from some form of autism. An early estimate was that in every 100 autistic individuals ten showed some high-level specific skill. However, it is now more realistically held that at most one or two in 200 of those within the autistic spectrum disorder can justifiably be regarded as having a genuine talent, though a reliable frequency estimate does not exist as yet. Savant talents are usually evident in the domains of number or date calculation, the visual arts and music; though, as I will also describe, there are some rare cases with high-level abilities in the area of language. Although savant talents do manifest themselves in such relatively few areas, they nevertheless represent a broad range of mental processes. Therefore such abilities should be viewed as more than an idiosyncratic collection of skills. However, these specific talents are usually of very little help to them in mastering the intellectual and social demands in other areas of life.

One of our first encounters with a savant occurred when during a visit in the late 1970s to an institution for mentally impaired people Neil O'Connor and I came across a low-functioning 13-year-old boy, whose reasoning ability was equivalent to that of a normal 4-year-old. The first thing he asked me when we met was the date of my birthday. When I told him it was 7 August, he said instantly, 'That was on a Wednesday in 1940, and in 2004 it will be on a Wednesday again.' I was stunned, and of course had no idea whether he was right. (He was!) All that we could establish on this occasion was that the boy possessed no calendar, but was obsessed with dates. The only calendar in this institution hung on the wall in the superintendent's office, and Mickey was fascinated by it, leafing through it whenever he had a chance. At this stage we didn't even know that there were such things as perpetual calendars and neither of course did Mickey. But subsequently we discovered that the Gregorian calendar is structured in accordance with certain rules and regularities. Knowledge of this helps calendar calculation, a feat which is normally well beyond the capacity of an ordinary person. Was it possible that this child we had come across had used these rules? We decided that we would find out.

On another occasion, we were in the classroom of a special school for children with severe learning difficulties. A colleague had drawn our attention to a very musical autistic boy who was a pupil there. It was Christmas time, and the teacher was playing carols on the piano in front of the class, trying to make the children sing along with the music. In the middle of the lesson she was called to the telephone and left the classroom. Suddenly Noel, who was then 15 years old, got up from his seat at the back of the class, went to the piano and sat down. He proceeded to play all the songs we had just heard, complete with the harmonies as well as the melodies, using both hands and efficient fingering. We asked him whether he had ever had any piano lessons. 'No.' 'Have you got a piano at home?' 'No.' 'Have you ever played the piano before?' 'Yes, sometimes here when they let me.' Later we were told that Noel spent much of his time at home listening to music on the radio, and the next day would play what he had heard on the school piano. You will hear more about Noel later on.

At yet another special school a child had entered the classroom rather late. 'Why are you so late?' 'Accident,' he replied. 'What sort of accident?' He did not answer but sat down and began to draw a brilliant picture of a collision between two cars as if seen from above. The headmistress told us that Stephen drew all the time and had an amazing visual memory. So we took him to St Pancras Station, a huge intricate Victorian building. He got out of the car and spent the next few minutes walking round the station. Later on that day he drew an amazingly accurate detailed picture of it from memory. When Stephen's drawings were shown to the late Sir Hugh Casson, who at that time was President of the Royal Academy of Art, he said that Stephen was the most gifted child artist he had ever encountered. Now Stephen has attended art school, and I will describe his experiences there later in the book.

Before Neil O'Connor and I began our investigation of the nature of savant talents in the early 1980s, most accounts of such individuals' outstanding abilities had tended to be purely descriptive. They told us what these people could do, but made little attempt to explain how those who were otherwise mentally impaired in various degrees could yet achieve these extraordinary feats. Such descriptions, fascinating and insightful as they often are, evoke wonder and amazement but convey little understanding. We thought that in order to obtain insights into the mental processes that underlie these specific abilities we would have to devise a controlled experimental methodology that would enable us to analyse them in some detail. This is what we proceeded to do.

One essential component of such an approach is the comparison of savants with normal people who are similarly gifted. Are the characteristics of specific talents (musical, numerical, artistic, etc.) of people who otherwise function on a low level of general competence of the same nature as the abilities of people without such handicaps? Is talent independent of intelligence and of mental impairments such as are seen in autism? And why are so many savants autistic?

To answer such questions, we not only need to define such terms as 'talent' and 'intelligence', and design well-controlled experiments, we also need statistical analysis. This is because the study of human behaviour, with which psychology is concerned, differs from other sciences because of the marked individual differences between people. The limited number of individuals that we can ever test may lead us to conclusions that cannot be generalised. We can therefore never be absolutely sure that the results which are obtained would be repeated with another group of individuals or with an altered methodology. All we can do is to find out how probable or improbable it is that our results are valid and reliable. In order to assess the degree of such probabilities we need statistics. Psychologists usually accept a finding as 'real' when there is a probability no larger than one in 20 that the results are just due to chance or to an uncontrolled factor. But of course one is more confident when the statistical analysis shows that there is only one chance in 100 of drawing the wrong conclusions from the findings. I need not go here into the technical details of how one determines such probabilities. All I will do is to try to make some of the reasoning clear and to point out that whenever I talk of 'differences' between groups of people, or those within one group where its members can solve some sorts of problem but not others, these are statistically significant differences. Those who are not interested in such reasoning may skip the following section.

When Tim, who is autistic, found the missing puzzle piece that no one else noticed, was this a fluke or does he really have a special ability to notice details? To answer this question we would give Tim a series of problems to solve. Solution of all these would depend upon noticing details. From this study we would get a measure of his ability to detect details, such as the proportion of problems that he can solve. If he can solve most of them we can rule out the probability that his answers are simply a matter of luck. This procedure is equivalent to tossing a coin to see if it is biased. If we toss it once and it turns up heads this is just chance, but if it turns up heads six times in a row, or ten times out of 12 throws, then we can be pretty confident that it is biased. (With a truly unbiased coin, we will throw six heads in a row on less than five of 100 occasions.) We also take it that such results are probably reliable. If someone else tossed the same coin or if someone else tested Tim's ability to detect details on another occasion, we could be pretty confident of getting similar results.

However, just because Tim is good at detecting details and is also autistic, we cannot conclude that the ability to detect details is a general characteristic feature of autism. In order to reach this conclusion, we need to test more autistic children and show that they are all (or at least the majority) good at detecting details. In addition, we need to demonstrate that they are better than normal children in this respect. Rather than testing just one autistic child, we need to test a number (say ten) and at the same time test a similar number of normal children. We can then compare the abilities of the two groups. We will gain some impression of that from the average or mean ability of all the children in each of the groups. However, this single mean is not enough. We also need to know how much the children within a group differ from one another. If some autistic children get very high scores on the tests of their ability to detect details, while others get low scores, then clearly being good at this task is not characteristic of autistic children. If we just considered the average performance of the group we might be misled. A high mean could result from one or two children getting very high scores while the rest performed at an average level. We need to use statistical procedures to decide whether or not groups differ from one another. These procedures take account not only of the differences between the mean performances, but also of the variation between performances of the children within a group.

Unfortunately we do not usually have access to a large number of autistic children from whom a few representatives can be selected at random. It might often be the case that our group of ten are all the autistic children we are able to examine. Our interest is to find out about behaviour on our tests that relates specifically to autism and not to some irrelevant factor that is not related to it. One of the most important of these factors is intelligence. Even though some autistic children have a good level of intelligence, a typical group of them will have an average intelligence level that is lower than a typical group of normal children. In order to be sure that our results are related to autism rather than low intelligence we need to compare our autistic children with a group of children who have reached the same state of mental development ('mental age') or have the same level of intelligence (IQ) but are not autistic. This is called a 'control group'.

Following such a procedure, one finds that children with autism are indeed better at detecting detail than those who do not suffer from autism but have the same general intelligence levels. In other words, these children show an unusual and uneven profile of performance across different tasks. They are usually good at some tasks, such as remembering train timetables, whilst they are usually bad, for instance, at remembering stories. To ensure that any such effects we observe relate to autism and not to other factors, we choose children for our control group who are matched with those who are autistic for their ability to remember stories. The key question then is how will the two groups of children perform with, for instance, a list of random words? When we do this we find there is a great deal of variation in the performance in both groups. At first sight it does not look as if we can find any true significant difference. However, if we compare each autistic child's performance on the two tasks, we see that all of those with autism do better when remembering random word lists than when remembering stories. There is no such systematic difference for the children of the control group. Here, statistical analysis shows a significant 'interaction' between tasks and groups. In other words, there is a performance difference between the two tasks for the autistic group but not for the normal one. In general, experiments in which groups of children perform more than one task, so that 'interactions' can be examined, are much more informative than simple group comparisons or performances on a single task.

But I must repeat that any statistical analysis only indicates the level of probability by which we might have been wrong to draw our conclusions. Psychologists usually accept a finding as valid when there is a probability no larger than one in 20 that we have obtained a chance result. Thus as I have said before, when I talk of differences between groups or within a group in the following chapters I will always mean a statistically significant difference of at least a 95 per cent probability that we obtained a true pattern of results.

A crucial issue already touched on is that the majority of savants not only suffer from some degree of mentally impairment, but are also diagnosed as being autistic. Following my long-term collaboration with Neil O'Connor, Linda Pring and I embarked on a fruitful and enjoyable cooperation which lasted for 10 years. Our joint work focused on the nature of this association between specific savant high-level abilities and autism. Autism is a rare condition, and the majority of those affected also suffer from various degrees of intellectual impairment. It was first identified in 1943 by Leo Kanner, and its main symptom is that the children who are affected fail to relate to other people. In Kanner's words, 'they treat people as if they were things'. He also noted marked language deficits in autistic individuals as well as a restricted range of interests, obsessions with unvarying routines, and insistence on an unchanging environment. He called this 'an insistence on sameness'. Various theories regarding this syndrome have since been advanced, but for present purposes I will only talk in some detail about one of these, the 'weak coherence theory', which will be outlined in chapters 2 and 3. This predicts not only deficits but also assets as a consequence of the style of autistic cognition, and for this reason it seemed to us to be the most relevant one for our research. Here, it is sufficient to say that there is as yet no recognised cure for autism. A probable cause is a presently unspecified dysfunction of the brain which is sometimes accompanied by epilepsy, and in many cases a genetic factor also appears to play a part.

This is a personal account of the research that my collaborators and I have carried out over nearly 20 years. I will therefore not review the extensive literature on this topic that our work has initiated. Others, such as Donald Treffert in his book *Extraordinary People*, have already done this much better than I ever could. What I will do here, is confine myself to describing those of our own studies that aimed to investigate the nature of the talents of savants who were gifted for foreign language acquisition, poetry, calendar and numerical calculations, the visual arts and music. We carried out such experiments with savants and with intellectually normal individuals talented in the same domain, as well as with those who had the same level of intelligence as the savants but no special abilities. In addition, this report will also include qualitative assessments of individual cases.

Two chapters describe and analyse rare savant talents in the area of language. One concerns a woman who is quite unable to deal with everyday events or to have normal social interactions (Chapter 4). She cannot solve verbal problems which any normal 8 year old can cope with, nor can she converse fluently; but she can write beautiful and evocative poetry. We compared her poems with those of a normal, highly intelligent amateur poet. The other case is that of a young man who as a child could not cope in a mainstream school and still cannot lead an independent life (Chapter 5). His conversation is very stereotyped, but he knows about 16 foreign languages and can learn a new one in a matter of weeks.

Two following chapters will deal with calendar calculators, this being the most frequently found ability amongst savants. Astonishingly, these individuals can quickly tell the day of the week on which a particular date in the past or future falls. This skill has sometimes been accounted for solely by practice, and certainly calendar calculators acquire and remember a vast number of individual dates. However, I will show that they achieve their extraordinary feats by also making use of the rules and regularities inherent in the calendar structure. I will then describe studies of the nature of their memory for dates that were carried out by our research associate Lisa Heavey.

In Chapter 8 I will report investigations with an individual who can tell within seconds whether any given large number is a prime number (i.e. it is not divisible by any other number except by 1 and by itself). We compared this savant's ability to identify prime numbers with those of mathematics students and were able to specify the kinds of strategy that were used. I will also discuss savant artists' ability to produce pictures (Chapters 9, 10 and 11). Each savant artist tends to have his particular personal style, some being skilled in using detail, space and linear perspective with unusual competence, while others produce atmospheric or surreal-istic pictures. Though highly gifted themselves, they usually do not show the slightest interest in the work of other artists, nor in the viewer's opinion of their own work.

Pamela Heaton, while working with Linda Pring and myself, demonstrated that cognitive strategies used for understanding music by those with autism but without musical skills, could act as possible catalysts for the development of savant musical ability. These studies also showed that, in many ways, autistic children's musical understanding is unimpaired even when they have no talent for making music. These findings might help to explain why so many musical savants are autistic. One of their particular gifts is to be able to play or sing musical passages after hearing them just once or a very few times. In 1887, for instance, Langdon-Down, after whom Down syndrome is named, described a boy in his care in an 'asylum for the mentally deficient'. This patient was taken to hear an opera for the first time in his life and could later remember and sing perfectly all the arias he had heard. I will show that musical savants can extract, remember and use musical structures – i.e. the 'grammar' of music (Chapter 12). In addition to being able to use this knowledge for reproducing what they have heard, they can also improvise, transpose and invent their own musical compo-sitions. Finally, I will attempt to draw together the results of our in-vestigations and suggest some tentative ideas about the underlying mental processes which contribute to the savant phenomenon.

It is undoubtedly true that such experimental methods as are at present available to neuropsychology are still too crude to allow us firm and valid conclusions about the nature of human talent, be it in the context of the savant phenomenon or in relation to the population at large. But these limitations need not prevent us from trying to find out not only *what* some people can do, but also *how* they do it. Thorndyke, an influential psychologist in the early part of the century, had asserted provocatively: 'Everything that exists, exists in some quantity and can therefore be measured.' Much of such attempted measurement will lead to over-simplification and subsequently will need to be revised, but it has the merit of being subject to such revision, confirmation or falsification. This research report tells how my collaborators and I initiated attempts to bring a scientifically based methodology to the investigation of savant talents. By taking this approach I do not want to diminish the wonder about the apparently mysterious, extraordinary abilities of those gifted individuals who are otherwise emotionally and cognitively impaired. Yet, I am also in sympathy with the musings expressed in one of Arthur Conan Doyle's accounts of the feats of detection by Sherlock Holmes that 'it is a capital mistake to theorise before one has any data'. Thus I hope that the data I am providing in the following pages will allow the reader not only to feel an enhanced sense of awe, but also to gain an increased understanding of the nature of the extraordinary achievements by idiots savants.

2

Talent and Intelligence

'After all,' said the Duchess vaguely, 'there are certain kinds of things you cannot get away from. Right and wrong, good conduct and moral rectitude have certain well-defined limits.' 'So, for the matter of that,' replied Reginald, 'has the Russian Empire. The trouble is that the limits are not always in the same place.'

This quotation comes from a short story by Saki. It can be applied equally well to the two terms in the title of this chapter. Everybody has some idea of what is meant by them, but their definitions are somewhat vague and their meaning may differ for different people. These words do not describe things that are appreciable through the senses; they are abstract concepts. We all share to a large extent the meanings of words such as dog, chair or garden gate. But this will be far less true of the meanings which each of us assign to such words as justice or patriotism. What is meant by a cup requires little discussion, but everybody is arguing now whether a brick wall, a stuffed animal or a dishevelled bed can be described as 'art'. To avoid such ambiguities here, I will briefly define how the terms 'talent' and 'intelligence' will be used by me in this book. I do not claim that the definitions I give have any general validity; they will simply clarify what I wish to convey when I use them.

Some lexical entries define being gifted as a 'faculty miraculously bestowed', and others as a 'natural endowment'. The biologist E.O. Wilson regards extraordinary achievements as being due to a quantitative edge in brainpower rather than coming about by magic or as gifts of God. There is clearly some truth in this, but such a view would make it difficult to account adequately for idiots savants, as by definition the general brainpower in most of them tends to be reduced. Even excepting Wilson's assumption, there is still a great deal that remains unexplained about the nature of talent in general and savant talent in particular.

When I use the term 'talent' in this book, I mean by this an inherent predisposition that is no more than a potential, but may serve somebody to become very good within a specific area of activity. This inherent potential is often, but not always, genetically determined. In any event, it is not easy to differentiate nature from nurture as key influences in many cases. Children who have musical parents may inherit that gift, but they will also be exposed to a great deal of music from an early age. They will thus acquire a relevant knowledge base. But others, who are musical but have neither gifted parents nor a stimulating environment, may spontaneously provide such experiences for themselves, for instance, by listening frequently to music on the radio. However, it is still not even clear to what extent exposure to an area is necessary at all for the emergence of a talent. Most savant artists, for example, tend to be uninterested in and do not look much at other people's paintings.

In the English language 'having a gift' has the same meaning as being talented, thus implying that a talent is something given to one, neither deserved nor asked for. But what an individual makes of such a gift is another matter. There has to be not only a natural facility but also an eagerness to learn the skills and techniques needed to play the violin or football outstandingly well. What is essential is both practice and the motivation to persist in trying to improve one's natural ability and to make the most of it. Does one have to be a particularly clever, fair or nice person in order to develop a given talent to a high level of achievement? No, one can be mean, unjust or even fairly stupid in many respects and yet become a brilliant pianist or racing driver. Peter Shaffer tackles this independence of great talent from personal worth in his play *Amadeus*, where the hardworking and competent composer, Salieri, is enraged by the genius of what he calls 'this obscene child, Wolfgang Amadeus Mozart'.

Some contemporary and influential psychologists hold that there is no need to presume the existence of inherent gifts at all, and that talent is not a real phenomenon, but a myth. They conclude that outstanding specific abilities are primarily due to continuous practice aimed at improving performances. However, among other contributing factors, such as early experiences and habits, those who hold such views also include preferences as a determining element, and one might thus ask what gives rise to such preferences in the first instance. Certainly as far as high-level specific abilities of savants are concerned, the spontaneous pleasure in the activity itself is palpable, as is the facility with which it is mastered. An account of outstanding ability in savants as being due primarily to goal-determined practice is unlikely to be the whole story, or rather it may be telling the story the wrong way round. It is highly improbable that savants persist in drawing, playing the piano or calculating dates because they want to improve their performance. They are usually quite indifferent to how these activities strike a viewer or a listener. It is more plausible that they keep on doing something that they are naturally good at because this gives them pleasure, such activity being its own reward. I think that this may also be so for many of us. We tend to prefer doing things that come easily and are fun because we have a natural aptitude for them. Relative ease and speed of such domain-specific learning is in fact one of the indicatiors of talent. Though it is a truism that practice makes perfect, practice alone will not do.

People with mental impairments are hardly good at anything unless they are lucky enough to possess a potential predisposition for something (i.e. a gift). They persist in the relevant activity because that gives them an intense satisfaction. Frequently, savants have no relevant environmental experiences available to them, and their talent often becomes apparent quite suddenly at a young age. People with limited mental capacities, as well as with a tendency for repetitive behaviour, as we find in those with autism, may concentrate even more on their natural special abilities than those who have more distractions available to them. One consequence of such preoccupations is that continuous repetition of a subject matter might help the gradual emergence of knowledge about its structural properties, though such knowledge may remain unconscious. Thus storing single items of information (e.g. remembering birthdays, as do many calendar calculators) is only the beginning. Gradually, through continuous repetition, the segments connect with each other and begin to form a coherent organised network. The rules that govern such an emerging knowledge base need not necessarily be verbally formulated. Nevertheless, some implicit learning of structural properties tends to occur.

In fact an extraction of structures can be transposed to other new tasks, as shown by the improvisations and transpositions by savant musicians. It was also demonstrated by one of our calendar calculators, and it is perhaps relevant in the present context to describe here a study by Linda Pring and myself which illustrates such flexibility of rule application to unpractised material. An incidental observation indicated that Peter, a calendar calculator, had linked the letters of the alphabet to the serial positions of the numbers 1 to 26. Given for instance the number 17, Peter would immediately supply the letter Q and vice versa. He might of course have practised these letter/number correspondences extensively for himself, so we decided to confront him with new sequences of the letter/number pairings with which he was unlikely to have become familiar.

In one of these studies not only one alphabet but a sequence of five of them, together with the corresponding numbers from 1 to 130, was briefly shown to Peter. In a number of trials which were carried out after this initial exposure, he was then asked to supply corresponding letters to randomly selected numbers as quickly as possible. He could do this easily and it took him for instance only three seconds to reply with 'P' to the number 68. In another experiment we reversed the usual letter/number correspondences so that Z became 1, Y 2, B 25, etc. We strung five such reversed letter/number series together resulting in a series of 130 pairs. Again, after having looked briefly at the display of the sequence and being asked to supply the appropriate letters to the randomly selected numbers, Peter's responses were all correct, though he was somewhat slower than a professional mathematician who acted as a control participant. However, all his responses were given in less than ten seconds.

Finally we presented both participants with a sequence in which the pattern of association between numbers and letters was variable. In all, three alphabets were used, but this time in the first and in the last of these the alphabetic positions were reversed in relation to the numbers, while this was not the case for the middle alphabet. Thus A corresponded to 26 in the first reversed alphabet and to 78 in the last one. However, in the middle sequence A was 27 and Z was 52. Peter was of course not told how this or any of the previous sequences were structured and had to work it out for himself. After a short exposure to this varied sequence, another set of 100 per cent correct responses were obtained from him. The professional mathematician made some errors but he quickly corrected these himself. Again he was faster than Peter, taking an average of five seconds for his answers compared with Peter's ten seconds. Nevertheless, the savant's error-free performance in all these three experiments is astounding and indicates a fast spontaneous grasp of hitherto unpractised sequential rules and relationships.

But although talent is defined here as a given potential to do a particular thing particularly well and thus not as a myth, it must be stressed that having such a gift is distinct from high achievement. Francis Galton wrote in 1869 that neither capacity without zeal, nor zeal without capacity was enough to obtain eminence. He did not think that even a combination of these two components was sufficient without the mental and physical power to do a great deal of work. The great painter Joshua Reynolds stated that if one had great talents, industry would improve them. He added however that if one had only moderate natural abilities, industry would simply supply their deficiency. Thus Reynolds thought that practice was no substitute for talent.

While talent usually manifests itself as a specific, quasi-modular entity, intelligence is understood to be a general capacity to deal effectively with all kinds of mental problems. Intelligence encompasses functions of understanding, knowing, learning, thinking, evaluating, planning and integrating information from different sources. That some people are inherently more intelligent than others is something that is now often regarded as being 'politically incorrect'. Nevertheless, it is indisputable that, largely because of their genetically determined potential, those who are more intelligent perform cognitive operations better than those with lower levels of intelligence. Thus environmentally disadvantaged children will usually catch up when their circumstances improve and will eventually reach their natural intelligence levels. Richard Dawkins, in his brilliant book *Unweaving the Rainbow,* writes that for some reason many people take grave political offence at the suggestion that some individuals are genetically cleverer than others. But he holds that this must have been the case when our brains were evolving and there is no reason to expect that facts will suddenly change to accommodate political sensitivities.

One way that is often adopted to deal with unpalatable and stubborn facts is to change the words that define them. Alan Clarke, one of the initiators of scientifically based enquiries concerned with the characteristics of mentally handicapped people, has provided me with a list of the terms used at different times to describe mental impairment. Here it is:

- fatuus naturalis

- idiocy

- oligophrenia

- dementia
- feeble-mindedness
- mental deficiency
- mental subnormality
- mental retardation
- mental impairment
- intellectual disability
- learning difficulty
- learning disability.

Clarke told me that as a joke he once added 'intellectually challenged' to the list. He was amazed to be told by his social worker students that this term was actually used in their work environment.

It is worth noting that psychologists distinguish between 'intelligence' and 'cognition'. While intelligence is considered to refer to a stable mental capacity, cognition is seen as an active process through which knowledge is acquired. Cognitive activities includes those of perception, attention, memory and learning. But the differences between these two concepts are subtle, and here I will use them interchangeably when referring to the general ability to think and solve problems. Both cognitive processing capacity and intelligence predict success in many areas of life, such as in educational and occupational achievements. Nevertheless, it is as well to remember that while intelligence is regarded as the relatively stable mental state, cognition refers to the processes involved in its manifestations.

So people undoubtedly vary with regard to their level of intelligence. But can such individual intelligence differences be measured and quantified? Yes, they can. At the beginning of the last century the French government asked Alfred Binet to develop a method of determining objectively the role that intelligence plays in predicting which children might or might not be able to profit from higher education. Binet went about this task without any theoretical pre-conceptions. He simply thought up a large number of questions and problems which he asked children to solve. He then selected those items which the majority in a particular age group could deal with. Such children, he considered to have an average level of intelligence. But he also found that some could deal with problems which were too difficult for the majority of their age group, while others could only manage at a level of difficulty typically already coped with by much younger pupils. He then discarded all the problems that did not differentiate between the children in this way and kept only the ones that did. And so the intelligence test was born.

If a child at a certain age performs in such a test similarly to the majority of those of his age group, he is thought to possess an average level of intelligence, which is quantified by expressing it as an intelligence quotient (IQ) of 100. However, if somebody aged eight can also answer the questions normally only dealt with by an average ten-year-old, such a child would have an IQ of 125 and a mental age of ten. He or she would thus be pretty clever. On the other hand, if a child in the eight-year-old group can only solve the same kinds of problems as an averagely intelligent six-year-old, his IQ would be determined as being 75 and his mental (as distinguished from chronological) age would be six.

In general the test worked then and it still does. The measured mental age (MA) reaches its maximum at the age of 16. The IQ remains broadly constant over time, so that somebody with an IQ of 125 when he is eight years old will tend to have a similar IQ when aged 18. He may thus do well at university, while a student with an IQ of 100 would have some difficulties and somebody with an IQ of 85 would not be able to cope at all. This has led some psychologists to state that 'intelligence is what intelligence tests measure'. There is some truth in this assertion; nevertheless, the IQ does rather reliably predict the degree of success in a number of important aspects of life. Thus, when I refer to intelligence in this book, I use it with reference to the intelligence quotients obtained from intelligence tests.

Even in his day Binet realised that intelligence measured in such a way is not a single unitary function, and he distinguished between 'perceptual' and 'verbal' intelligence. These refer respectively to problems presented and solved through language and those which are presented visually and require spatial reasoning. However, by and large, people who do well with verbal reasoning will also be rather good at solving visuospatial problems. There are three basic classic accounts of the nature of intelligence, and the more contemporary theories put forward are to a greater or lesser extent derived from these. In 1904 Spearman stated in an article called 'General intelligence objectively determined and measured' that there was indeed such a general factor which he called 'g'. However, he also found that while some mental functions depended strongly on 'g', others did so only partially, and some abilities did not depend on general intelligence at all. Thus this 'two-factor theory' postulates a general factor 'g', which contributes to different mental processes in varying degrees, and an 's' factor, specific to particular types of functional skill (i.e. mathematical, numerical, etc.).

In the 1930s Thurstone suggested the presence of 'group factors' such as perceptual speed, numerical manipulation, verbal fluency and comprehension, as well as spatial conception, memory and general reasoning. However, the general factor of intelligence was still found to be the major contributor in determining the level of efficiency at which these group factors operated. Then in the late 1940s and early 1950s Jeffry Thomson's 'anarchic' theory denied all existence of general intelligence. He thought that there were only areas of specific mental functioning, each with its own potential to develop domain-specific intelligent behaviour. The apparent generality of intelligence was, according to him, simply the result of separate mental processes sharing the same neural pathways. These accounts have all been extended and re-analysed and have become more detailed and sophisticated. However, as I have said, most contemporary accounts remain essentially based on one or other of the above assumptions regarding the nature of intelligence, and for our purposes we need not go into them here.

In relation to savants, the relevance and nature of intelligence has been discussed by Leon Miller, who wrote one of the earliest and best accounts of musical savants. Assessing the available evidence, he concludes that of all the savants that have been investigated half in fact had IQs below 75, that is below the average range, while the other 50 per cent of cases fell into the low normal range of intellectual functioning on at least some sub-tests of intelligence. However, the degree of excellence shown by an individual in his particular domain was independent of his level of intelligence. Though such intelligence independence seems to apply more to the areas of art and music than to numerical and linguistic abilities, this is perhaps not too surprising, as something similar appears to apply to the population at large. Thus in one classic study students at the mathematics faculty of an American university had the highest IQs, while those studying the arts had lower levels of intelligence. (I am not sure that it is actually wise to mention here that psychology students were also found to score relatively low on intelligence tests in comparison with those studying other science subjects.)

In this context it is relevant to take into account that the majority of savants are autistic, and that it is characteristic of such individuals to show 'islands of intelligence'. Their IQ profiles are more uneven than those of other mentally impaired people. Furthermore, the sub-tests in which autistic individuals without special talents tend to do well are the same as those in which savants also excel. Thus, one could possibly conclude that it might be the autism-related component functions of cognition that are evident in savants' intelligence test results. It should also not be forgotten that intelligence differences between gifted normal people exist as well. Although some painters or musicians may be generally much brighter than others, this need not influence their modular, domain-specific level of excellence.

In regard to theories of the nature of intelligence in the context of savant ability, the most influential as well as the most relevant of such more recent theoretical accounts is that proposed by J.A. Fodor in *The Modularity of Mind*. Taking up and extending Spearman's position, Fodor holds that the mind contains two kinds of structure, which he calls the 'modular' and the 'central'. Modules draw their specific information from the different senses, such as sight, hearing, touch, etc. These sensory-based systems are modular as they are each domain specific, fast, self-contained and encapsulated. The modules do not share their information with each other, but pass it on to a central system. This system is general, interactive, draws inferences and integrates as well as interprets the information it has received from the modules. The central system also forms concepts, enables abstract thought, and is not too different from Spearman's general intelligence. So far, so good. But Fodor also thinks that the language function is a self-contained, encapsulated module, and this proposition is simply not tenable. It is of course true that language has a sensory basis, but there is much more to it than that. It is clearly also a central process, as it is propositional, contextual and communicative. Neil Smith, a professor of linguistics, and his colleague, I.M. Tsimpli, have therefore called language a 'quasi-module'. O'Connor and I put forward a similar view in regard to domain-specific talents. For instance, a specific gift for art, music or mathematics tends to be self-contained, as are Fodor's modules, but it also includes its own aspects of central processing. Particularly in individuals with general mental handicap or mental impairment, talent-related cognitive operations remain restricted to the area of special ability. We could thus regard savant ability as 'quasi-modular', i.e. being circumscribed by, but not restricted to, sensory-perceptual processing.

The approach which we have taken in the research to be recorded here was to investigate whether savants' specific abilities were associated with aspects of the particular cognitive characteristics that are typical of autism. Does the cognitive style that is distinctive of individuals with this syndrome influence certain qualitative aspects of the talents themselves, and the routes and strategies employed in their development and manifestations? In order to answer such questions one has to compare savants not only with others of the same mental levels but without specific talents, but also with normally functioning individuals with similar specific abilities as the savants. Thus, where appropriate, we have carried out studies that included such control groups. This has enabled us to isolate those aspects of talent-related mental features that are shared by savants and similarly gifted normal people alike. In addition, we have also carried out single-case studies in order to learn about the underlying strategies used by individual savants in the areas of their high-level abilities. This may seem a rather pedestrian and mundane approach to anyone aiming to understand the conundrum presented by the idiot savant phenomenon. However, as others have pointed out before me: when confronted with a complex puzzle, scientists seek to solve it by turning not to the Lord but into the lab. I hope that the reader may be prepared to accompany me along this path.

3

Autism and Special Abilities

In 1943 the psychiatrist Leo Kanner published an account of an 'autistic disorder' that he had observed in some of his child patients. I have to include a description of autism here, because most of those who have an outstanding ability in spite of other mental impairments are diagnosed as being autistic. As this is a much rarer condition than general mental handicap, we will have to ask what may be the reasons for this predominance of individuals with autism among the savant population.

The Greek word *autos* means 'self', and Kanner believed that the inability to make close emotional contacts with other people was the central symptom of autism. This lack of responses to others shows itself very early in life. Autistic children will, for instance, not stretch out their arms to be picked up and will retain a rigid body position when held close. Babies will not respond to smiles and as Kanner observed when he saw them later, 'they treated people like things' – a child with autism might step on another on the floor as if it were a lifeless object.

Psychologists differ somewhat in their interpretation of the causes of this unrelatedness to others. Some see it as a cognitive inability to acquire what is called a 'theory of mind'. This term refers to a growing awareness by the normally developing child that other people have their own thoughts, beliefs and feelings and that these are not always the same as those held by himself. Autistic children are much less able than others to 'mind read' in this way.

Other psychologists think that the reason for what Kanner called 'autistic aloneness' is rooted in an emotional rather than in a cognitively based unconnectedness with other people, which is unlike the normal child's almost instinctive social responsiveness. The eighteenth-century empirical philosopher David Hume held that all normal people were by nature sensitive to the feelings and beliefs of others, but that had nothing to do with their capacity to reason. However, it may be a somewhat unproductive question to ask whether people's social responses are primarily an expression of feeling or of thought, as in this respect these two systems surely interact with each other.

Kanner noted other symptoms of autism, such as an 'obsessive desire for sameness', resulting in the children's insistence on fixed, repetitive routines and on an unchanging environment. Thus the mother of an autistic boy related that after having bought some new knives and forks, her son got so upset that she felt obliged to put the old ones back in the drawers. This need to preserve sameness and predictability can go to remarkable extremes. One child I met went so far as to insist on walking only in the same direction from which he had set out. When his mother began to turn a corner into a side street, he threw himself onto the pavement screaming and refusing to turn with her.

To those with autism the ever-changing aspects of life at every level seem to present themselves as an unpredictable chaos over which they have no control and which has little meaning. This often leads to the adoption of rituals that are reassuring. To a much lesser extent we can also see something similar in the occasional behaviour of many normal children. I myself remember that for a time I felt compelled to touch every second lamp-post for luck. Like Christopher Robin, I also did not allow myself to step on the lines of the pavement, but jumped from square to square so that the bears around the corner would not pounce on me. But it was only a game I played, and deep down I knew that the magic I associated with such games was not real, but created by my imagination. For children with autism, to whom nothing much appears to be real or makes sense anyway, something unpredictable and frightening may actually seem to lurk, something that has to be kept at bay by rituals and repetitive routine.

As Kanner noted, this insistence on sameness by those with autism goes together with a very restricted range of interests. Some autistic children get obsessed by phone numbers and will endlessly enquire about them. Others are fascinated by train timetables, or will know all the kings and queens of England, or all the flags and currencies of countries. But if it so happens that they have an inherent predisposition to be good with numbers, or music or drawing, their interest will naturally focus on such an area, and they will be eager to continue pursuing such activities as are related to their special ability. As I have said, we all enjoy doing what we are good at and therefore tend to do it often, thus getting even better at it without much effort. In fact, a facility for such effortless rapid learning is regarded as one of the hallmarks of talent. An autistic child who is good at very little, yet can master one particular domain, will of course be drawn to focus even more on behaviour related to such an isolated potential than a normally developed one, who has many distractions available to him.

One feature which Kanner noted was that autistic children had excellent memories, seemingly out of line with their frequent general learning difficulties. They remembered strings of apparently unconnected items particularly well, and this memory capacity will become relevant when we will talk of the nature of autistic savants' talents. Kanner also observed deficits in the area of language. These children began to talk late and some did not learn to speak at all. If they did, their language was extremely concrete and literal, so that they could not understand jokes and irony, or interpret metaphors. One of our collaborators told me of a rather intelligent autistic boy, whom she saw sobbing while waiting in the lunch queue at his special school. When asked what was wrong, he pointed to the menu written on the board which offered 'marble cake'. He said unhappily, 'I cannot eat this, marble is much too hard.'

Soon after Kanner had published his first account of autism, the Austrian paediatrician Hans Asperger published his independent description of an apparently similar syndrome. Like Kanner, he thought that an inability to relate to other people was a central inherent feature of autism. But though he also noted other very similar symptoms such as Kanner had observed, his sample also differed in marked and important aspects. Asperger's patients included those who were rather intelligent and in particular showed good language ability. He even reported an unusual freedom and originality in language use by some of his patients. He went so far as to describe them as 'abstract thinkers' and thought that they performed best when allowed to behave spontaneously. Nevertheless, these individuals also had great difficulty in coping with normal everyday events and social interactions. Psychiatrists now distinguish between Kanner's 'classical autism' and 'Asperger Syndrome'. They speak of an 'autistic spectrum disorder', where people may exhibit different symptoms in different combinations and to various degrees of severity.

A vivid account of the experiential similarity of Asperger and Kanner syndromes was published by Therese Jolliffe, an outstandingly intelligent person who had nevertheless suffered from all the symptoms of autism. She has a doctorate in psychology, did research at a leading university and now studies medicine. She writes that as a young child she never thought about or missed her parents or brother when they were absent. She did not realise they were supposed to be more important than, and different from, other objects. She recalls that she liked to open and close boxes and the doors of her toy cars over and over again, and watched fascinated as she turned the wheels round and round. Many children with autism enjoy turning, twisting and spinning things and, like her, are also fascinated by some sights and sounds, while fearing others. Therese also put her toys into long rows, rather than playing with them by pretending that they were real. This absence of 'pretence play' is characteristic of autistic children.

Therese reports that she finds it difficult to look at people's faces even now, especially their eyes. She says that autistic people do not so much withdraw from reality as never really understand what this is in the first place. There is nothing for her to withdraw from, as reality is a confusing jumble of events, people, objects, places, sounds and sights, without clear boundaries. There is little meaning in anything she encounters, and thus set routines, rituals and repetitions help to get order into an otherwise distressingly chaotic world. Her intelligent insights confirm Kanner's original description of autism, as well as Asperger's observation of high intelligence and language ability in his patients.

In 1963, while working for the Medical Research Council, Neil O'Connor and I began the first long-term experimental investigation of the thoughts and language use of autistic children. Before we embarked on this project, hardly any controlled investigations with autistic individuals had been published, although there were a number of interesting case reports. But nobody had sought to determine, for instance, which of the behavioural features observable in those with autism were a consequence of impaired intelligence and which were specific to autism. Also, on some tasks those with autism seemed in fact to do better than non-autistic children with the same levels of general intelligence. We thus introduced the inclusion of non-autistic comparison groups into our studies, who were matched for IQ with the autistic participants. In other experiments, the controls were normal children who were considerably younger than those with autism, but had reached a similar level of mental development as the older, but less intelligent autistic participants. In 1970 our book *Psychological Experiments with Autistic Children* was published and as some of its reported studies are relevant in the present context I will briefly mention these here.

In one experiment, we compared autistic with non-autistic children with the same IQ levels for their ability to recall words. In some of these sequences the words were randomly strung together, while in others they formed a meaningful sentence. An example of the first kind of material would be word strings like 'drink, church, cloud, green, run'. In the other condition, the participant would be asked to recall the same number of words but in the form of a sentence like 'ride home by car now'. The overall frequency at which the words occurred was the same for both types of material. We found that though all children remembered sentences better than non-sentences, this was significantly more marked for the non-austistic participants than for those with autism. Thus this autistic group's recall scores in the two conditions were much more similar to each other than those of children with the same IQs who were not autistic.

In that early study, the two types of word strings to be recalled had differed in two aspects. First, one had coherent meaning while the other had not. Second, one but not the other had a grammatical structure, i.e. it was a sentence. We thus had to ask ourselves whether it was the absence of meaning or syntax structure that appeared to matter less for those with autism.

To disentangle these two variables, we carried out two further studies. In one of these, remembering sentences that made sense was compared with those that did not. Examples for the two types of sentences included 'gentle frames eat angrily' or 'nice children play happily'. We found that this only made a significant difference for the non-autistic participants, who recalled the nonsense type of sentence much less well than the one that was meaningful. This was not the case for those with autism. In the second study, we used a characteristic of normal memorising which is called 'conceptional clustering'. When hearing a number of words like 'white, green, five, blue, black, eight, two', after a little while people will not be able to recall all these words, and will also not remember them in the order in which they have heard them spoken. Instead they will say something like 'two, five, white, black, green'. They have clustered the words in their memory according to their conceptional categories of numbers or colours. They also might erroneously include numbers or colour names that had in fact not been presented. This was the way in which the non-autistic participants in our study responded. But for the autistic children there was no such clustering effect and no conceptual intrusion errors. They repeated the words in the exact order in which they had heard them spoken.

It was the great British psychologist, Sir Frederick Bartlett, who demonstrated that we tend to obtain and recall a general impression of things and events. On this basis we then construct, often incorrectly, the probable details. We tend to go for the 'gist' of things, while autistic individuals tend to ignore this. The results from our experiments on the short-term memory of autistic individuals seemed to indicate that it was primarily the meaningful aspects of language processing that were impaired.

We concluded that we regarded such an inability to encode stimuli meaningfully as being a basic weakness of autistic cognition. Moreover, as the intelligence levels of the two groups we had used in our studies had been the same, this deficit appeared to be primarily due to autism, rather than to low intelligence. Subsequently others replicated and extended such findings. From a series of important studies, our colleague Uta Frith concluded that 'weak central coherence' was a basic cognitive characteristic of autistic individuals. As I have said, this term referred to a bias of those with autism towards focusing attention on parts and details of information rather than on an integrated perception, cognition and memory. Thus those with autism do tend 'not to see the wood for the trees'.

Suggestions of a normally predominant tendency to discern wholes rather than their components was first put forward by the Gestalt psychologists (the German word Gestalt means 'configuration'). They demonstrated that we have a strong and compelling bias to perceive such coherent whole configurations rather than parts and local details of a display. Even with simple shapes as, for instance, a square, it needs an effort not to see this as a single Gestalt, but as four separate lines each at right angles to the others. Shah and Frith discovered that those with autism found it easier than non-autistic participants to resist such compelling wholistic information processing. In an ingenious study, they used a version of the 'block design test' where it had been repeatedly observed that autistic people perform better than expected. A picture showing a total pattern has to be reconstructed from separate blocks, each showing fragments of the total. In their study, the patterns were presented in two forms.

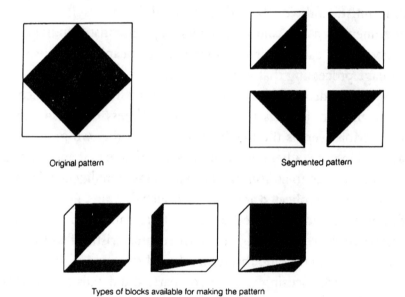

Original pattern   Segmented pattern

Types of blocks available for making the pattern

Figure 3.1 Block designs

In one condition the model pattern is seen as a total configuration and in the second it has been 'pre-segmented' into its constituent parts. When the non-segmented pattern had to be reconstructed from the blocks, the autistic participants could do this significantly better and faster than those without autism. When, however, the model design was shown in 'pre-segmented' form, the advantage of those with autism disappeared. Shah and Frith concluded from such results that a facility of those with autism to segment wholes into their constituent parts was a consequence of 'weak central coherence' in autistic individuals.

Basing her conclusions on such results as a superior performance on this block design test, as well as on other related findings, Francesca Happé has proposed that weak central coherence did not so much represent a deficit but rather a particular cognitive style. She concludes that such a style typically adopted by those with autism was evident on the perceptual, the visuospatial-constructional as well as on the verbal-semantic levels. On the perceptual level, for instance (though there are also contrary findings), she reported that hidden shapes in a drawing that are overlaid by a larger, structured design are more easily detected by those with autism than by those without. People with autism seem to focus on the separate parts of such design, rather than on its dominant coherent aspect. Autistic people's constructional superiority on the block design test has already been cited, and on the semantic level there is powerful confirmation of weak central coherence from the findings of a study by Frith and Snowling. They found that autistic children took no account of context when reading out sentences containing words that were spelt the same, but were pronounced differently according to their meaning. Thus 'she had a big *tear* in her dress' was read out as if it was 'a big *tear* in her eye'.

Weak central coherence on a semantic level is also demonstrated by an anecdote cited by Happé. She tells of an autistic child whom she tested for his ability to name objects. When describing a picture of a bed the child said quite accurately: 'This is a blanket and this is a sheet.' 'And what is this?' the experimenter asked, pointing to the picture of a frilled pillow. 'This is a piece of ravioli' was the answer. This was certainly a response out of context. But some psychologists investigating 'creativity' have suggested that such 'field independent' and 'diverse thinking' (i.e. forming unusual and unexpected associations) shows the workings of an original mind. Asperger would have agreed with this and would probably have taken such a far-fetched association as a piece of ravioli on a bed for a sign of what he called 'spontaneous thought', not restricted by conventional and contextual boundaries. Although 'creativity' should be regarded as an ability to 'make or do something' rather than a state of mind, could such a tendency of 'field independence' in autistic perception and thought play some part in accounting for the fact that most savants are autistic?

Due to improved diagnostic tools and the broadened definition of autistic spectrum disorder, and also because of the inclusion of Asperger Syndrome, the number of those diagnosed as being autistic has risen. But it is still a rather rare condition; one thus has to ask why, in spite of this, the majority of those with an above-average specific ability in spite of some mental impairment suffer from some form of autism. In a recent survey of the relevant literature, Leon Miller found that between 70 per cent and 80 per cent of savants had such a diagnosis. In our own sample of about 50 savants, between 80 per cent and 90 per cent were autistic or suffered from Asperger Syndrome.

Of course, no single theoretical framework could satisfactorily account for such a multifaceted condition as autistic spectrum disorder. Nevertheless, the 'weak central coherence' theory is the only one about autistic perception and cognition that allows not only for mental deficits, but also for certain assets that may result from such style of information processing. It might thus be the case that for gifted autistic individuals the route towards achievement could lead from an initial focus on details and segments to the eventual production of integrated pictures, music, calendar structure and even poetry and knowledge of foreign language. It was this hypothesis that served as a starting point for Linda Pring and me in our investigations of the nature of autistic savant talent.

4

Poetry

Fragments mend
make for
genius
fragmentation
when normal thinking
would give up.
The pieces find the resource
within

bits of the whole
puzzled jigsaw,
my self.

This poem is by Kate, who was diagnosed by the psychiatrist Lorna Wing, a leading expert in this field, as suffering from Asperger Syndrome. In this condition autistic symptoms are present, but a relatively high level of cognitive functioning is preserved. As I said in Chapter 3, such people tend to see the world as a jumble of unconnected fragments. The cited account given by Therese Jolliffe described this state of mind better than I ever could. But here is Kate, transforming such jumble into a meaningful whole by turning it into a poem. Kate, who is now in her forties, started writing poetry only when in her twenties. Linda Pring and I heard about her from a friend and supporter who knew her well. This is how he described her to us:

> Kate knows and understands a great deal but seems to have very limited ability to structure. To use her way of putting things, her life is a heap of odd-shaped stones. Anything she tries to construct soon falls down, whereas other people build amazing structures, which often seem impenetrable and meaningless walls to her, hemming her in on every side. The more structured a subject, the less it means to her, but even cause and effect at a simple level can be very shaky. Large lumps of life are unpredictable if they step outside her learned rule of thumb, and chaos hovers ever present in the background.

Such a state of mind supports the diagnosis of Asperger Syndrome as described in Chapter 3. Diagnosis was made on the basis of the responses to questionnaires especially designed as diagnostic tools; the responses confirmed Kate's lack of friends since childhood. There were problems in understanding other people's feelings and points of view. Kate did not make eye contact and repetitive speech as well as obsessional fixation on certain restricted topics were observed. Stress in response to some sounds and fascination with others were evident. There was a tendency to collect and cling to certain classes of objects, and attempts to maintain 'sameness' in the environment. Ann Dowker of Oxford University had previously worked with Neil O'Connor when she had analysed the poems of young children. So Linda Pring and I asked her to co-operate with us in investigating Kate's poetic gift. In the account given here I was greatly helped by the comments and criticisms of Adrian Pilkington and by his publication on the analysis of 'poetic effects'.

The German writer Mathias Altenburg has said that the writings of an author must always be cleverer than he is himself. In this sense a poem, just like a picture or a piece of music, assumes an autonomous existence, representing its own self-contained truths. This is of course especially relevant to the productions by savants, which to a considerable extent do appear to be independent of their generally limited mental competence.

Here we have attempted to compare Kate's poems with those of another amateur poet, whom we will call Emma. While Kate has considerable mental impairments, Emma is highly intelligent. But they share some degree of physical handicap, as Kate suffers from a relatively mild form of cerebral palsy and so does Emma. In Kate's case this results in some loss of manual dexterity, making her rather clumsy. She has an awkward gait and often uses a wheelchair. Emma also has some difficulty with walking and uses a stick. She also has some hearing loss. In a poem of her thoughts about these difficulties, Emma says:

> ...*I am afraid*
> *Of many things. Of my anger:*
> *have known too long it cannot change*
> *those things I would most spend it on.*
> *Save it for nothing, and the rest*
> *I've learned to hide. So many things;*
> *and love the longest fall I fear...*

In regard to their effective cognitive level of functioning, our two poets are very different. Kate first went to a school for mentally handicapped children. When she was later transferred to a mainstream 'secondary modern' school, she was unable to take part in the lessons or cope with the social demands. She spent most of her time sitting silently at the back of the classroom, and never made friends with the other children or played with them. In contrast, Emma was a high achiever at school, gained a degree from a leading university and on a verbal intelligence test she obtained a very high IQ of 133. When, however, we tried to test Kate's verbal reasoning ability, she seemed not to understand the test questions and we could not reliably establish an IQ. She could not or would not say, for instance, in what way an apple and a cherry are alike (both fruits). She also gave some odd answers on a test for understanding the meaning of words, saying that 'coil' meant 'retreat' (confusing it probably with 'recoil') and that 'pitch' meant 'field' (perhaps thinking of cricket). However, as mentioned earlier, such diverse associations have been taken by some investigators as indicating 'creativity'.

Kate is not interested in, nor does she read, other people's poetry. She seems not to appreciate irony, which is associated with thought attribution. She also does not understand jokes or teasing, and this leads to a frequent misunderstanding of other people. She is unable to cope with the simple practical aspects of life, needs continuous help and support and now lives in a sheltered community where she is looked after. Her speech as a child was reported to be repetitive and fixated on a few particular topics, a characteristic with autistic features. Some monotones and odd intonations in speech were also observed. At the present time, her grasp of the meaning of words in daily verbal intercourse is very literal, and she has a limited range of facial expressions. On a formal test of social maturity she functions like normal five to eight year olds, and her daily living skills are at about the eight-year level. Yet she writes poetry which clearly shows depth of thought and reflection. Here are two poems, one by Kate and one by Emma, about themselves. Perhaps the reader would like to guess the author of each poem. Here is the first:

> *my lameness my stumbling*
> *are not there to be disregarded*
> *take them make them*
> *into myself and so see me...*

and this is the second:

> *Here I give a finger: it's got no hand.*
> *I've got a face: I never saw it.*
> *I touch a leg: didn't see the rest.*
> *Here I be: must have gone somewhere.*

Gave a daisy: nothing else.
Got lost in clothes but not the body.
Sent my eyes into what I do.
Feet tip-a-toe: quick I was then not.

I sat in heaven: the ground went.
Sing come in: a sound got shouts.
Screaming holes got no edges.
I'm a something where fog lingers somewhere.
No one comes where I go.
I saw death when help came faster.
The fish had no water.

The first verse is by Emma and 'The fish had no water' is by Kate. This contradiction between Kate's incapacity to cope generally (often misunderstanding what other people say) and her ability to write like this is strange, isn't it? But the savant phenomenon *is* strange and contradictory. This is another of Kate's poems:

Big strong, white belted cows,
I adore looking at you,
To put my arm across your bold girth,
Working across a wide field together,
chewing grass simultaneously like rain
on a sunny day with the blue of the sky.
They look at you slowly and calmly.

Their tongues would caress you as
they come near if you sit with them,
lying down in the heat of the day,
eyes looking at you in curiosity,
all together knowingly belong.

In this poem Kate not only makes use of the rather infrequent word
'girth', but she also appears to cross the mind barrier between
herself and other creatures, a barrier commonly associated with
autism. Yet in her poem, she gives the impression of having some
thoughts about what it is like to be one of the cows. The next two
poems are also by Kate.

Spiral, spirals, round and round,
coming to the same place,
nothing getting out;
in and out, over and under, through;
this way and that, up and down,
interlocking me to slam back,
putting me in knots;
everything ending where it started,
emptying, unvitalised, choked in spasms.

Can I ever stop the chaos,
crippling my intentions
to mere fragments shapelessly,
helplessly into senseless connections?

Will you ever listen?
spirals end up dying desperately,
in my head of agonising torture.
My body pushes circles away
from my soul,
to see a chink of light that is mine
in ever increasing circles.

***

Words missing;
directing links lost:
every now and again
a word pops up
within my head

that helps.
Months go by;
the connection
just connects
when I say it in right place,
leading it to right person.

She goes
'Ah, is that what you meant?'

In attempting to account for poetic effects, Adrian Pilkington has pointed out that due to individual differences between poets, and also because of historical and geographic influences, elements contained in poetry shift and differ in emphasis. For instance, some languages make rhyming more appropriate than others. Nevertheless, some formal patterning such as recurring elements, metre, alliterations and other sound effects are all found in various forms of poetry. In the following analysis, we compared the poems by the mentally impaired individual with Asperger Syndrome, Kate, with those of the highly intelligent but also physically handicapped poet, Emma. We looked at their poems' thematic content, as well as at the use of poetic techniques and devices, such as phonological patterns and rhyme, and we also noted the use made of metaphors. Pilkington proposes that one attempt to account for poetic effects in cognitive terms is to explore the contextual references that are made by such metaphoric figurative language.

We analysed about 70 poems by each author. When considering what these poems tend to be about, we find some differences in the extent to which their respective handicaps dominate their themes. About half of Kate's poems are concerned with such self-analysis and self-reflection, as is evident in those quoted earlier. But in a quarter of Emma's poems, like that cited before, this theme is also dominant, and many poets may write about their problems, inner state of mind and their own selves.

In view of Kate's diagnosis of Asperger Syndrome, it is interesting that the frequency of poems dealing with personal relationships is identical for Kate and Emma. For each of them, about 20 per cent of their poems tackle this issue. Those by Kate reflect her sense of failure in this respect, as can be seen in the following verse:

> *but your mouth*
> *is closed*
> *to me.*
> *Silent silence*
> *between us.*
> *Did it end*
> *when I was not looking?*

A poem by Emma on this theme contains the lines:

> *but you – or I, who knows? –*
> *won't let me come too close*
> *and I in my ill-slung frame of bones*
> *am reduced to words*
> *to draw you to myself.*

When it comes to describing other people, we find Emma doing this much more often than Kate. She writes of a relative:

> *...Aunt Nan was eighty-seven when she died.*
> *I don't know how, but I see her*
> *slipping out in amethystine twilight,*
>
> *smiling, rigged out with stars*
> *in her white hair.*

But Kate can also write on this theme, as in a poem called 'Derelicts':

Naked as stone,
a powerful skull,
hunched over,
uncomfortably asleep;
imprisoned in humps,
hollows full of lumps,
the shapeless derelicts
in local park.

Emma describes landscape and nature more frequently, though Kate does it too when she writes:

Dry, white stone walls,
Vision of beauty
In the dales I love
Sun reflects through the holes of age...
Smooth, rough, flat, round, knobbly, white stone.

A poem by Emma on this topic contains the verse:

Below the chalky wave of cliffs
five patterned fingers clenched on grey
seen among pebbles catch the eye
long ago sea urchin laid under sand
slow crystal movement, calcium to flint
leaves only the folded star to shine
single from the countless stones.

T.S. Eliot, in a talk on 'the three voices of poetry', has said that the first of these was of the poet talking to himself – or to nobody. This is the voice predominantly used by Kate. She is rarely concerned with the other two voices mentioned by Eliot, those of addressing an audience or making an attempt to create dramatic characters. But primarily the poems do reflect the two writers' personalities and life experiences; we concluded from this content analysis that their themes probably did differ no more than would those of any other poets who in some respects have similar problems to deal with.

Our next aim was to look at some of the formal poetic devices used by our two poets. But before going into more detail about this, it should be mentioned that while thematic content on its own gives no information about artistic quality, neither does an account of formal patterning alone tells us much about poetic effects. The prominent linguist R. Jacobson has suggested that some of the aesthetic impacts of a poem are due to an innate desire for regular symmetric patterns, such as are inherent in rhyme and metre. However, Pilkington points out that approaches based purely on such text-internal features can explain verse but not poetry. He suggests that one needs to focus on mental representations and processes which poems evoke and which are specific to poetic communication.

However, starting our analyses with such text-internal devices, we found a marked difference between the two poets in the frequency with which they used sound-based or rhythmic features, such as rhyme, alliteration or metre. Emma does this much more than Kate, who does not explore such techniques to any great degree. But though Kate uses these devices sparingly and only about half as often as Emma, she does write lines such as 'my tears of years'.

Another text-internal device called 'modified repetition' is syntax based so that a sentence form is repeated with different words slotted into the same sentence frame. Kate does this in the poem below:

> I was contradicting my own patterns
> very intelligently
> till society <u>hit</u> me.
> I knew my own patterns to create much
> leisure, pleasure, safety,
> till society <u>whacked</u> me.

I knew how to start
to control the input,
slowly giving confidence,
to my own upward surge powerfully
till society heavily bounced on me.

Both poets used such modified repetition equally often and Emma writes in a poem called 'Cantelon' as follows:

King and Queen of Cantelon
Is it so far to Babylon?

Yes, Babylon is far away.
You'll not get there by light of day,
But strike your foot against a stone
And you may come to Cantelon.

I strike my foot against no stone,
I will not come to Cantelon.

Oh Babylon by candlelight,
You'll get there if your feet are light,
But strike your foot against a stone
And you will come to Cantelon...

Next we considered the occurrence and nature of similes and metaphors in the poems by Emma and Kate. Such figurative expressions serve as symbols or representations for something else and are central to poetic effects. In a simile, a direct comparison is made, as for example, 'a heart as hard as stone'. In a metaphor, a word or phrase is linked to another to which is not literally applicable, such as 'I fell through a trap door of depression'. Adrian Pilkington has argued that an exploration of metaphoric context will contribute to a cognitive theory about what creates true poetic effects. Figurative language is of course not confined to poems, but Pilkington is concerned with the contextual exploration of metaphoric use in poetry. A conventional stereotyped metaphoric expression like 'Sue is a pest' evokes only one possible interpretation, namely that Sue is awful and should be avoided at all costs. But of the American poet Walt Whitman it was said 'that he laid end to end words, never seen in each other's company before', thereby evoking new and wide ranges of contextual meanings and references. Thus the less contextual and the more open to various interpretations a metaphor is, the greater the possibility of its evoking complex mental responses. Emma writes:

> The cicada's rough constancy of noise
> shrills through the night
> a sound like water falling.

This is a simile rather than a metaphor. In Kate's earlier cited poem 'Derelicts' she uses rhyme as well as simile, and her poem 'Fragments Mend' cited at the beginning of this chapter essentially consists of a single extended metaphor. But she makes perhaps the most poetic metaphoric use in her poem about cows, where working together in a field whilst simultaneously chewing grass is linked to rain on a sunny day with a blue sky. This leaves the reader to explore for himself her possibly referring to the simultaneity of pleasure and toil. It is the ambiguity of metaphoric references that creates poetic effects. In contrast, Kate's metaphoric line 'The fish had no water' serves unambiguously to express her inability to function in, and communicate with, the world in which she finds herself. Only one contextual interpretation, that of despair, is possible here; nevertheless, the metaphor is still quite vivid and powerful. All successful art will evoke and communicate cognitive reference as well as feeling states. Wordsworth has written in his preface to the *Lyrical Ballads* that poetry represents a spontaneous outflow of feeling. Pilkington points out that, to achieve the successful poetic communication of such feelings, the least obvious, least stereotyped references will result in the most powerful poetic effects. But even with her limited grasp and ability to search consciously for such representations, Kate succeeds nevertheless in communicating her sadness and despair about her limitations through her poems more powerfully than would be possible for her in a context outside this domain.

What is noteworthy here is that in Kate's case both talent and impairment are evident within the same function, that is in language. She cannot, for instance, understand, use or define words which are frequently used in ordinary speech, though in the context of her poetry she employs a large vocabulary. But perhaps such discrepancies are not that surprising. Even our everyday experience tells us that the efficient use which somebody makes of language may vary with his interest and expertise in regard to what is talked about. A barrister fluently arguing a case may not find equally evocative words to describe a spring day, and a politician making an eloquent speech may not be able to martial similarly convincing words about matters outside the realm of politics. Kate has great difficulties in appreciating the thoughts, feelings and attitudes of other people, yet in her poem about cows she manages to communicate a sense of 'cowness'.

Metaphors have not always been regarded as an essential element for the creation of poetic effects. Their frequent use is a relatively modern phenomenon; the philosopher and poet, Friedrich Nietzsche, was one of the first, in the late nineteenth century, to point this out. He drew attention to the then modern tendency of substituting figurative language and metaphors for words that derived directly from sensory-perceptual experiences. The modern Greek poet Dimitri Amalis takes up this point. Rejecting the use of bold metaphors, he says: 'I have walked too long in the hinterland, where myth unloads the symbols of life.' In his poetry he aims to match external reality with an equally object-related language.

Pilkington has remarked that Kate's poems seem to him like early drafts rather than fully finished productions, though they contain the elements of poetic ideas. Probably the same could be said of many of the drawings and paintings that savant artists produce, or of the improvisations by savant musicians. Perhaps one reason for savants not aiming 'to get it just right' is because what they do serves them primarily as a means of self-expression rather than communication. But of course it is also the case that critical assessment does play little or no part for savants in the production of their poems or pictures or music. There is no aim for the greatest possible perfection. Notwithstanding such qualifications, against the background of her social and intellectual impairments, Kate's poems are remarkable. In her case, as well as in others that will be discussed further on, it becomes clear that specific functions, as in this instance language, cannot be regarded as unitary, at least not in savants and probably also in other people. Rather, these functions appear to be subdivided into quasi-modular sub-domains.

The poet Seamus Heaney said in his Nobel Prize acceptance speech that poets aim to represent concrete reality as well as to follow the inner laws of a poet's being. In a minor, modest way, and in spite of her poems' limitations, Kate attempts to do just that when she writes about 'big strong, white belted cows' and also:

> *I lost the me*
> *It got under everything*
> *That was not poems*

5

Foreign Languages

Christopher can understand, talk, read, write and translate from Danish, Dutch, Finnish, French, German, Greek, Hindi, Italian, Norwegian, Polish, Portuguese, Russian, Spanish, Swedish, Turkish and Welsh. Yet when briefly attending a mainstream school he could not cope with class work and was held to be mentally handicapped. He is now aged 37 and is unable to lead an independent life. He lives in a sheltered community where he works in the garden, and he is continuously keen to learn new languages. He has a loving and caring family who take him on holiday trips abroad, and he seems content with this life.

His mother was over 40 years old when he was born, and had contracted rubella early in pregnancy. Oxygen was administered at birth, and the baby subsequently had feeding difficulties and was observed to throw his head about a lot. He started to walk and talk late, had a mild speech defect and poor eyesight. He was also said to have made strange noises at night, and at the age of two he was judged to be mentally retarded. Later, he attended a centre for handicapped children and then went on to a special school for the 'educationally sub-normal'. His motor co-ordination was poor; for instance, he could not catch or throw a ball or cut his nails. When aged 20, he was described as suffering from 'severe neurological impairment of his motor co-ordination'. A recent brain scan has revealed moderate diffuse brain abnormalities not infrequently found in relatively high-functioning autistic individuals.

When he was given an intelligence test at 14, his performance on perceptual-spatial problems was only comparable to that of a normal eight year old, but his verbal IQ was at the average normal level of just below 100. On a scale measuring mental maturity, his scores were similar to that of normal nine year olds. He could not deal well with numbers and, for instance, would be unable to estimate whether he had been given correct change in a shop. He could not master a classic 'conservation of numbers test', in which he was shown two pieces of wire, on each of which the same number of beads was strung. When the beads on the two wires were aligned, Christopher judged the number of beads on both strings as being the same. But when these beads were spaced out on one string while on the other they remained adjacent, he consistently said that whatever line was longer contained more beads than the shorter one. Normal children can conserve numbers in such conditions by the age of five. But from the age of three he is reported to have read newspaper advertisements and to have picked up some French from his elder sister's schoolbook. He showed a love for books, though those he preferred were not the usual children's stories, but telephone books, dictionaries and those listing flags and currencies of countries. He actually dislikes fiction and fairy stories.

Though Christopher has never been formally diagnosed as suffering from autism or Asperger Syndrome, he does show most of the behavioural features associated with these conditions. He tends to avoid eye contact with other people, and hardly ever shows any strong emotions apart from his delight and enthusiasm in anything to do with foreign languages. He does not engage spontaneously in general conversations, and when a testing session ends he tends to get up without another word or glance and leaves the room. In spite of his normal verbal IQ, like others with autism or Asperger Syndrome he fails to understand irony or jokes. He also cannot understand metaphors, and he responds in a manner typical for those with autism to situations where it is necessary to appreciate other people's states of mind, thoughts and beliefs. In one test that investigates such 'mind reading', a toy is put into a drawer while two children are watching. Then, while one of them leaves the room and the other one remains, the toy is removed from the drawer and hidden behind some books. The remaining child, who has watched this, is then asked 'When your friend comes back, where will she look for the toy?' A child with autism will usually answer 'Behind the books'. She cannot dissociate what she herself saw and knows from what her friend will think and believe. Some of Christopher's responses to such 'theory of mind' tests showed a failure to appreciate that other people's state of mind may differ from his own. But in contrast he could judge that others might have a different physical viewpoint from him. When, for instance, sitting at a table with another person sitting opposite him, he could appreciate that a scene of toy houses, mountains and trees placed on the table at eye level may look different to him than to his opposite. He realised that the houses he saw in front of the high mountains would be obscured by them from an opposite point of view.

Neil Smith, a professor of linguistics whose investigations of Christopher's astounding foreign language acquisition will be reported in this chapter, gives a telling example of his typically autistic disability to appreciate pretend play. Smith said to him that as a joke he would act as if he were to ring up a friend by telephone. He then picked up a banana and put it to his ear saying 'Hello, hello, are you there? How are you?' When he asked Christopher what he had been doing the answer was: 'Putting a banana in your ear.' Question: 'Why was I doing this?' Answer: 'I dunno.' Normal three year olds do understand such pretend games, but Christopher did not.

When Neil O'Connor and I first met Christopher he was friendly though somewhat laconic and withdrawn, and despite his normal verbal intelligence level we found it quite difficult to involve him in ordinary conversation. However, as soon as the talk turned to foreign languages his face lit up and he became happily animated. Up to that time his foreign language ability had never been formally assessed but was simply described in anecdotal reports. For instance, soon after Christopher began to attend his special school, a teacher had noticed that he seemed to understand some Polish. When asked how he happened to know this language, he replied that he 'just did'. But in fact he has a Polish brother-in-law and had heard him talk in that language. He is able to pick up a language from any source that offers itself, listening to the radio, obtaining foreign newspapers, or being formally taught. He acquires a new vocabulary and the morphology at an astonishing speed and without any apparent effort, though he has more difficulties with new grammars. When dealing with question-and-answer tasks in a newly acquired language, he prefers to do this in written rather than spoken form.

On an early visit to Christopher's special school, an Israeli teacher told O'Connor and me that over a five-day period, she had shown and read out to him 300 cards, 60 each day. On each of these cards a printed English word was paired with its equivalent in Hebrew written in Latin script. When on the sixth day after this the teacher tested him by showing all the English words he had seen before, she reported that Christopher could supply nearly all the corresponding Hebrew ones after the single previous exposure. However, in a similar test carried out more recently by Smith and Tsimpli he made several mistakes, though his performance was still impressive. Once when we went to see him, we were accompanied by a French colleague. As soon as Christopher discovered this, and as I had told him before that my native language was German, he took great delight in switching from one of these languages to the other, though the content of this conversation was still very repetitive and stereotyped. Everything to do with foreign languages gives him intense pleasure, and he is endlessly preoccupied with this topic. However, it remains true that what he has to say in any of these languages, including his native English, is very limited.

Of course, we were familiar with accounts of some people's abilities for rapid and extensive foreign language acquisition. But as

far as I am aware, up to the time Neil O'Connor and I began to investigate Christopher's astonishing skill, there had been no reports
of a comparable competence by someone with his mental limitations. The archaeologist Heinrich Schliemann, who made such
important discoveries in Troy and Mycenae, apparently acquired
about 15 languages in the three months before he set out on his first
expedition. The British historian Macaulay is reported to have had
the same facility, and other such gifted linguists are described in the
Encyclopaedia Britannica. According to one such entry, Mithridates
of Pontus, who lived from about 120 BC to 63 BC, knew 25
languages and James Chrichton (1500–1585) had learned ten
before the age of 15. These examples pale in comparison with
Cardinal Giuseppe Mezzofani (1774–1849), who seemed able to
speak 50 languages and translate from 114, and Sir John Brown, a
British diplomat who reportedly spoke 100 languages and read in
200. However, to what degree each of these languages was
mastered is unknown, and it is advisable to be somewhat sceptical
about the accuracy of these anecdotal accounts.

Neil O'Connor and I began our investigation of Christopher's
linguistic talent by giving him a standard English vocabulary test
that indicates how many words a person understands. Each page in
a booklet shows four pictures, each one illustrating a different
object, action or concept. The person being tested is then told a
word, and asked to point to the one picture of the four which illustrates it. The test starts with words that occur very frequently in
speech and are therefore familiar to most people, such as 'chair',
'running' or 'fruit'. The test gradually proceeds to more rarely used
words, for instance 'statue', 'sulking', 'senile'. On this vocabulary
test Christopher obtained a score that was equivalent to an IQ of
121. Though not outstanding, this is pretty high, and taken on its
own it would easily have qualified him for entrance to university.
However, on a test of verbal reasoning his IQ was only 89, which is
at the low average range of intelligence. Thus it was evident that his

knowledge of words was greater than his ability to use other aspects of his native language.

After having established the extent of Christopher's native word knowledge, we presented him with equivalent German, French and Spanish vocabulary tests. On the German test his IQ was 114, on the French 110. On the Spanish one his IQ was 89; though lower, such a score is still within the normal range for a native language vocabulary.

Next, we asked him to translate for us passages of texts in the same three languages taken from A-level exam papers, into English. Here are the three texts:

French text:

C'était le jour de la rentrée. Ce matin-là, je me suis reveillé à six heures, comme à la maison. Je suis allé coller mon oreille à la porte de mon cousin. Il respirait doucement. Une heure plus tard, j'ai sauté du lit et après m'être habillé, je suis entré dans sa chambre. Il m'a dit que je ne devais plus frapper à l'avenir, que c'était ridicule. Je me suis assis dans un des fauteuils et j'ai attendu. Au bout de quelques moments, Robert m'a demandé de lui préparer un café, qu'il a pris au lit.

Quand je le quittais pour aller au lycée il n'a fait que sourire. Arrivé à l'école, je n'ai eu à me présenter à personne, mon père avait tout reglé. Naturellement les autres élèves voulaient savoir mon nom.

German text:

Martin war jetzt zu Hause angekommen. Die Wohnung war klein und befand sich im vierten Stock des Gebäudes. Er schloss die Tür von innen ab und ging in die Küche, wo er schnell ein Glas Wasser trank und sein Paket in dem Wandschrank verschwinden liess. Sein Herz pochte immer noch vor Angst und er trat mit leisen Schritten in sein Schlafzimmer. Am Fenster schaute er vorsichtig auf die Strasse hinunter. Erst konnte er niemanden entdecken. Bald bemerkte er jedoch vor einem kleinen Blumenladen zwei Männer, die in seine Richtung hinaufblickten. Seine Verfolger wussten also, wo er wohnte.

Spanish Text:

Visiblemente complacido, carmelo se ajusto las gafas, dio media vuelta y entreabrio las puertas correderas que communicaban con la pieza immediata, una habitacion espaciosa, con una potente lampara, sin pantalla, en lo alto, pendiente de una moldura de escayola, y una gigantesca mesa debajo, alrededor de la cual se sentaban, en sillas desiguales, una veintena de muchachos cuyos rostros se difuminaban entre el humo de tabaco. Hablaban todos al tiempo y sus voces se confundian con la del televisor sobre una banquete minuscula, en el rincon que formaba la pared con la puerta de acceso al vestibulo.

Christopher read out these three passages in English without any hesitation as if they had been written in his own native language, and he took less than a minute for each one. He made a few errors, some of them grammatical and others changing the sense of the sentence. Like on the vocabulary tests, his Spanish translation was less accurate than those from French and German. We then established that our linguist could answer questions asked of him in Russian, Hindi and modern Greek, as well as tell us a short story in Spanish after seeing it illustrated by four pictures. Though again he made some syntactic errors, he accomplished each task rapidly and competently, thereby demonstrating that his language ability went beyond simply translating into his native language.

At this point, we decided that an investigation of Christopher's extraordinary talent for acquiring foreign languages needed more expertise in the subject of linguistics than we possessed. We therefore decided to ask Professor Smith from University College London Linguistics Department whether he would be prepared to follow up this unique case of savant language talent. He agreed, and he and his colleague Maria Tsimpli have proceeded to study the nature of Christopher's language ability in depth. I asked Professor

Smith to allow me to include a simplified account of some of this research here, and he gave his consent. Thus the following summary of some of their studies are the only ones described in this book in which my collaborators and I have not directly participated.

Smith and Tsimpli began by investigating Christopher's native language ability in detail. They tested not only his ability to deal with spontaneous speech and conversation as well as syntax and meaning, they also studied whether he could make logical inferences from dialogues by, for instance, telling him: 'A boy called Fred asked his friend John "Do you speak Portuguese?" John answered that he spoke all the European languages.' Christopher was then asked whether he thought that John could speak Portuguese and replied with a 'yes'. It was clear that he could deal with all such relatively simple aspects of his native language, thus demonstrating integration in general language information processing.

Smith and Tsimpli also tested Christopher's understanding of metaphors. That is of particular interest, as people with autism generally cannot cope with these very well. Kate the poet, described in Chapter 4, is an exception to this, though her use of metaphors is restricted to her poetry. Usually people with autism or Asperger Syndrome tend to be very literal and concrete in their speech and understanding, like the little boy who thought 'marble cake' was too hard to eat. Christopher also showed such limitations when asked to explain the meaning of statements such as 'No man is an island' or 'Standing on the shoulders of a giant'. His response to what such statements meant was a puzzled 'I don't know'. Thus he, as well as most other people with autism or Asperger Syndrome, seem to lack an understanding of what one may call 'interpretive language use'. Such incomprehension also includes irony, jokes, rhetorical questions and other metalinguistic language aspects. In spite of such limitations, Smith and Tsimpli concluded from their extensive investigation of Christopher's native language ability that overall it was at the same level as that of other average native speakers. Their interpretation of certain apparent shortcomings was that these were not due to a specific deficit in the language domain, but were to be explained by Christopher's limited level of general intelligence and to an impaired functioning of his central cognitive processing system.

Next, the experimenters asked Christopher to translate texts from the 16 languages listed at the beginning of this chapter. Very few professional linguists would be able to do this, but Christopher could accomplish it at speed and without difficulty. However, fast and fluent as he was, he again made errors, just as O'Connor and I had already observed in our much more limited study. A striking observation was that when mistranslation occurred, Christopher did not seem to notice or care whether what he said made any sense. He appeared not to be concerned with the meaning of the whole sentence, but went about translating the text word by word, as if each stood not in a context but on its own. He treated a passage as if reading out each word from an internal dictionary, proceeding, as the researchers put it, 'like an automaton'. Moreover, when they asked him to take his time and look at the whole sentence first, he became distressed and said that he could not do this. Such a strategy towards focusing on single elements of language and disregarding context was found by Frith and Snowling to be characteristic of autistic children's reading of texts. They would often mispronounce homographs, i.e. words that are spelled the same but pronounced differently according to their meaning in a sentence.

In another interesting experiment, Smith and Tsimpli followed up the mismatch between Christopher's verbal and visual-perceptual intelligence test scores. He was shown displays of words in which the letters were not completely printed out, only fragments of each of them were visible. This was compared with his ability to recognise pictures of incompletely drawn objects where only fragments of the outlines were presented. There were 20 examples of graduated display for each type of material. They ranged from showing a minimal part of the outline of either words or pictures, through partly and not yet totally complete representations of them, to the fully written out words or complete picture contours.

The results showed first that Christopher did much better with words than with pictures, as he needed much less complete information for word than for object recognition. Also, when compared with normal control participants, he was the second best at recognising words when provided with minimal letter outline, but by far the worst when asked to identify incompletely outlined pictures. These findings were reminiscent of those that Neil O'Connor and I had obtained from savant artists. We had asked participants from four different groups to identify incompletely drawn objects. One group contained savant artists and the second normal art students. The remaining two were matched for their respective IQs with the two gifted groups. First, minimal fragments of line drawings of objects were exposed, and when identification was not possible on such a first exposure, other fragments of the drawing were gradually added.

Both artistically talented groups needed to see significantly less of the picture outlines to identify what was represented than did the intelligence-matched control individuals. We had interpreted these results by suggesting that the normal as well as the savant artists showed a faculty for constructive imagery derived from an internal 'picture lexicon'. This explanation accords with that given in regard to Christopher's outstanding ability to access lexical items. Thus it seems that for those gifted in a specific domain, information that is of relevance to their talent is stored in the form of internal representations which are very readily activated. From the results obtained by Smith and Tsimpli as well as by us, this privileged access appears to be independent of whether partial information is given in the form of incompletely written words, as in Christopher's case, or as incomplete pictures shown by us to those gifted in drawing. Moreover, the formation of such talent-related internal representations and their ready access appears to be independent of general intelligence, as shown by savants as well as by intellectually normal talented people.

Another important finding by Smith and Tsimpli was that Christopher's astonishing facility was not restricted to acquiring new words, but also extended to morphemes. Morphemes are the smallest identifiable parts of words as meaningful units that cannot be further divided (e.g. *wel, com* and *ing* from *welcoming*). There are also indicators of functional relations, and these differ in different languages. For instance, in English, with the exception of *to be* (i.e. *I am/you are*), there is no distinction between first and second person singular (*I* and *you*), and the verb form. Thus it is *I go/you go*. But there is a suffix for the third person (*he, she*) added to the end of the verb (i.e. *he goes*). In German on the other hand, there is general person-verb agreement as in *ich gehe, du gehst, er geht*. But in Berber, which is spoken in Morocco and neighbouring countries, person-verb agreements may vary from suffix to prefix. Thus the agreement pattern for first person singular has the verb suffix *gh*, while the second person has the prefix *t* in front of the verb stem, as well as a suffix *t*. For the third person singular, the verb prefix is *y* for masculine and *t* for feminine. When Christopher was taught Berber, a new language for him, he was able to produce correct agreement forms for such variations after a brief explanation and only two relevant examples. He took this up with pleasure and enthusiasm, and his morphological grasp was significantly better than that of normal comparison individuals. This was in contrast to his relatively flawed acquisition of new syntactic rules, where his performance was inferior to that of the controls. There he tended to transfer the grammatical parameters of his native English to foreign languages, to which of course they did not apply.

From these results, as well as from evidence obtained from teaching Christopher an invented artificial language, Smith and Tsimpli confirmed their conclusions that his linguistic strength lay primarily in the speedy and correct acquisition of apparently unlimited vocabulary items, as well as of the smallest structural parts (morphemes) of new languages. But his syntactic errors indicated that he appeared to 'filter' new grammars through the parameters of his native English. This was still the case after he had become quite familiar with another language.

How can we account for Christopher's limitations in acquiring new grammatical rules, when he can use comparable ones competently in his native English? And why is he at the same time outstandingly able to learn an apparently unlimited number of new words, as well as unfamiliar patterns of prefixes and suffixes, but unable to master the intricacies of syntax? Part of the answer could lie in the different ways in which we acquire words and grammar when we first begin to understand and use language. Names of things, activities, events and concepts are usually learnt. A small child might not know what the word dog means unless he sees a dog or at least a picture of one and is told or hears that this is a dog. He may also pick up vocabulary items from hearing them in context. But one does not spontaneously generate the commonly used correct labels for things one has never come across, though for young children the learning of such new words occurs at great speed.

But grammar is different, because it is 'generative'. As the influential American linguist, Noam Chomsky, has pointed out, 'grammar grows in the mind' and children's acquisition of syntax is intuitively generated rather than learned. As far as we know, all human languages comprise an indefinite number of possible sentences, governed by a finite set of rules. Though these rules differ in the way they govern different languages, they do fulfil a similar set of functions in all cultural contexts, such as making statements, asking questions, giving orders or describing things and events. Noam Chomsky holds that all humans are genetically endowed with a specific syntactic language faculty and all children in all environments are born with this. Thus, the human brain is 'hardwired' for the knowledge of the principles of 'universal grammar', and once syntactic parameters are set in a particular language, this allows for the intuitive analysis and production of identically structured new utterances and their meaning.

In his book *Noam Chomsky: Ideas and Ideals*, Smith does much to clarify Chomsky's quite complex concept of 'universal grammar'. As Chomsky holds that language is a genetically determined system in which all syntactic possibilities are laid out in every child's mind and brain, all children in any language environment have only to set the particular appropriate 'switch' and syntactic acquisition of their first language follows automatically. Thus, for instance, English (but not Japanese) has a word order of subject–verb–object (e.g. 'I eat fish'). Once heard, the appropriate switch is set and the child can now generate sentences that follow this rule such as 'I want bicky', though he may never have heard this phrase spoken before. As soon as children can decode the meaning conveyed in 'I like this', Smith says that 'all further structural knowledge comes for free'. The child will now generate utterances such as 'I eat this'. Thus children do not have to 'learn' that in English prepositions precede their objects as 'in the house, near the tree'. Consequently, when native language parameters have been set, large parts of the acquisition of syntax follow spontaneously and automatically.

However, when we set out to learn new languages later in life, we have to reset the syntactic rules and parameters we had intuitively acquired for our native language. For second languages, one has to learn consciously about new grammatical rules and their application. Thus the learning of second-language grammar is qualitatively different from first-language acquisition. For them one needs, as it were, to insert 'new software', 'a new program' to replace the initially given hardwired one, which seems difficult for Christopher.

On the other hand, his fast and seemingly unlimited ability to learn new words and morphological relationships (i.e. small local parts of a structure) appears to rest on similar effortless processes as those in young children's native word acquisition. What is special about his linguistic talent is that when he comes across a word in one language, it enables him directly and automatically to access its equivalent in all the other vocabularies he knows. He can 'read them all out' as from an internal multilingual lexicon. It seems possible that such a privileged access to self-contained verbal and morphological units could at least in part be accounted for by his tendency to adopt a cognitive strategy that is characteristic for those with autism and Asperger Syndrome. Thus he tends to focus on local elements, rather than on the structural and semantic aspects of new languages. This leads him to adopt a word-for-word translation and to transfer word order from English to other languages. One simple example of this, given by Smith and Tsimpli, was that when asked to translate the question 'Who can speak German?' into this language, he produced '*Wer kann sprechen Deutsch?*' instead of the correct '*Wer kann Deutsch sprechen?*'. Consequently there is a discrepancy between his seemingly unbounded ability to acquire new vocabularies and his limited skill in setting new grammatical parameters. It is words which serve as the building blocks for his astonishing foreign language ability.

The other issue is to what purpose Christopher puts his outstanding language acquisition skills. His object is neither communication, nor the expression of thoughts and observations which tend to be the main uses to which language is normally put. His aim of acquiring new languages is simply their acquisition, a process in which he takes an enthusiastic interest and intense delight. Christopher's talent, like those other savants who are gifted in music, calendar calculations, the visual arts, and so on, illustrates that such domains do not represent a unitary function, but contain 'sub-universes'. This distinction within compound components of mental operations is highlighted in savants. But they may perhaps also have wider implications for the nature of talent in general, as well as for the organisation within functional areas of the human mind.

6

Calendar Calculations

'What is time?' asked St Augustine. Imposing a structure on its flow has been an aim throughout history. During the Stone Age and for a long time afterwards, it was the moon that acted as the guiding light for measuring time. D.E. Duncan's lucid book *The Calendar* tells us about its history. It outlines that the moon passes through its phases from one new moon to the next during a period of between 29 and 30 days, and this phase takes exactly 29.53 days. Consequently a lunar year of 12 months has 354.36 days. The Greeks, who like other ancient cultures used a lunar calendar of 354 days in a year, had thus to add an extra 90 days every eight years to correct the progressive inaccuracy.

But already in about 4000 BC Egypt, one of the earliest civilisations, had turned to the sun, noting that the solar year was very nearly 365 days long. The Egyptians adopted a calendar of 12 months, each of them having 30 days, and the god Toth added five days to the year which were marked as the birthdays of various gods. Toth controlled the measurement of time and the calendar, and was also the ruler of the sacred ibis birds. These appeared and disappeared with the annual flooding of the Nile, which was the most important event of every successive year. Time was measured in number of floods (years) and these were always accompanied by large flocks of ibises. The regularity with which the Nile flooded determined the cycle of life in Egypt and acted as a natural calendrical timing device. Eventually, Egyptian astrologers realised that the solar year was in fact a fraction longer than 365 days and added another quarter of a day to the year.

When Julius Caesar came to Egypt, where during his prolonged stay he had a love affair with Cleopatra, he became familiar with the Egyptian solar calendar. He realised that the sun was the most powerful timepiece for the earth. After his return to Rome he initiated a change from the Roman lunar calendar to the solar one, which after some adjustments became the most accurate one in existence at that time. Caesar changed the beginning of the year from March to January. His calendar had 12 months alternating between 30 and 31 days, and he introduced leap years. In his system, February had 29 days in a normal year and 30 in a leap year. As we know, this was subsequently changed again. Further alterations were made by Constantine in AD 312, which included the introduction of a fixed date for the assumed birth of Christ (i.e. Christmas), while Easter remained a movable feast, still being determined by the Jewish moon calendar. But apart from minor corrections and alterations, the Julian calendar remained in operation until it was again reformed by Pope Gregory in 1582.

Because of the drift of the calendar year, Caesar had introduced one day to be added every 125 years, but by the sixteenth century counting the year had become ten days out of step with the true seasonal cycle. Gregory removed these ten days in one fell swoop simply by eliminating 5 to 14 October in 1582. The Gregorian calendar was soon adopted by most European countries, though in Britain and America it was only accepted in 1752. Our present Gregorian calendar is still subject to drifts resulting in inaccuracies and is running 20 seconds shorter than the solar cycle. By the year 4909 it will be a full day ahead of the true solar year.

I hope that this much abbreviated account of the history of our calendar has illustrated how the structuring of time has always been a human preoccupation. Such a preoccupation in its extreme form characterises the savant calendar calculator, and calendar calculation is probably the most frequently observed ability in savants. In a recent survey of the literature, Leon Miller found more than twice as many reports of calendar calculators than of either musically or artistically gifted savants. Calendar calculators are able to identify, usually within seconds, on which particular day of the week a specific date fell or will fall. They are intensely interested in dates and often the first question they will ask someone is not 'What is your name?', but rather 'When is your birthday?' This, for them, is the most important information they need about other people. While collaborating with Linda Pring and myself, Lisa Heavey met one calendar calculator who refused to work with her until he got such information not only about herself, but also about all the members of her family as well. 'When is your sister's birthday?' he asked 'Is she married?' When told she was, he wanted to know when the husband's birthday was and also asked his age. After he was told this, he informed her that her brother-in-law was born on a Saturday. Only when he had elicited birthday information about all members of her family was he prepared to co-operate with her further. On subsequent visits over several years this savant always remembered these relatives' respective birthdays.

Of course specific dates and times may become important not only to savants but to everybody. While, for instance, trying to solve a particularly tricky crime, Colin Dexter lets his Oxford detective Inspector Morse muse that though a flash of perception of unified time amounts to more than the sum of its parts, for solving his problem he would have to take account of often overlooked specific time elements such as particular days and dates. However, he needed to do this for a purpose, while for savant calendar calculators it is an end in itself.

In most savant calendar calculators, their ability manifests itself spontaneously in childhood. Thus one mother told us that once when they were on their way back from holiday, their eight-year-old son forwarded the information that they had stopped at the same restaurant three years earlier, 'and that was on 29 July, on a Thursday'. When asked a question such as 'On what date of the week was 2 January in 1876?' this savant will now respond by naming the weekday within seconds. When we asked him how he could do this, he answered: 'I just know.' Some calendar calculators will give their answers instantly, others may take 20 to 30 seconds or even longer for remote dates. The span of the years over which they can calculate also varies considerably between individuals. In a few cases they have a range that goes little beyond five years. Most of them can calculate across the present century, as well as over the ones before and after that and in other rarer instances savant calculation span covers many hundreds or even thousands of years.

How do they do it? This skill is rarely found in normally functioning people, though it does occur. Neil O'Connor and I once met a visiting Australian professor of history, who told us that as a child he and his father played a game where one of them asked for the day of the week of a particular date, which the other then quickly supplied. They could do this over a span of many hundreds of years, though the boy was never explicitly taught by his father any rules of this game. He also could not remember ever consciously practising this skill. Like the savants, he said that he could just do it when a child. It was this early interest in time that later played a major part in his eventual decision to study history. But this is a rare case, and while we often know ordinary people who can play a musical instrument, can draw well, or have a special ability for dealing with arithmetic, have you ever met anyone who was a calendar calculator? What does this fascination with calendars tell us about the savant mind?

As set out at the beginning of the chapter, our calendar is a highly structured, self-contained, rule-governed and repetitive system. It seemed possible to Neil O'Connor and me that these very characteristics might appeal to some autistic individuals who have an interest in dates and have also some, though not necessarily extensive, arithmetical ability. One might go so far as to suggest that similar qualities as those governing the calendar are also dominant features of autistic cognition. A system that reflects a rigid structure, repetition and regularity might therefore have a specific appeal for autistic individuals. Could it be that savant calendar calculators extract, though not necessarily consciously, the calendar's repetitive structures and regularities, and then use these in their calendar calculations? Nobody had ever made such a suggestion and it had never been tested before.

Some investigators had thought that visual imagery might play a part in calendar knowledge. According to this, the savant simply looks repeatedly and over very long periods at calendars and remembers this information in the form of visual images. Though this might possibly play a part in some cases, it will not do as a universal explanation since there are congenitally blind savant calendar calculators, and Neil O'Connor and I had indeed found one such participant in the group we studied.

Another more plausible proposed strategy is that of establishing 'anchor dates' or 'benchmarks'. Some savants might remember, for instance, on what day of this year a birthday, Christmas, or the start of a holiday fell, and then use this as a starting point for further calculations. Such anchor dates certainly have a role to play. The history professor I mentioned said he used such benchmarks now. He knew the date and day on which President Kennedy had been shot some years back and calculated dates prior or subsequent to this event from there. Such precise event-related memory can also be observed in some savants' calendar calculations, and this lends credence to the assumption that benchmarks do play a part in their calendar calculations.

Another favourite explanation for calendrical skill is simply in terms of memory resulting from extensive rehearsal. But the psychologist Horowitz, who studied a famous pair of twin savant calculators, discovered that one of the two could give the days of the week of dates over nearly 40,000 years. This span of time and the items it contains did of course far exceed the possible study of calendars that he could have practised and memorised. But even so, memory for individual dates based on excessive practice is a main explanation still favoured by many as accounting for this savant ability. Thus Ericson and his colleagues taught a group of university students to calculate dates simply through extensive and prolonged practice and memorisation. But this does not of course indicate that the ability as shown by savants is a result of the same procedure. Intensive teaching of university students does not imply that the same route towards achievement is taken by savant calculators or indeed by anybody with an inherent predisposition for a certain kind of activity. With instruction and much deliberate goal-directive practice most of us can learn to draw in perspective or play a piece of music on the piano. But those talented in such domains can do this spontaneously, though of course practice will also improve their performance. Thus while not disregarding any or all of the mentioned variables for improving performance, these do not provide a sufficient and reliable account for the underlying mental processes that are involved. To elucidate these, one needs to study groups of people with calendar calculation ability, and introduce control conditions concerned with other activities, in order to be able to conclude whether offered explanations have any general validity.

Seven of the eight participants in our group of calendar calculators had been diagnosed as being autistic, and the remaining one showed marked autistic features in his behaviour. Their IQs ranged from 38 to 88, that is from those with severe mental handicap to others who functioned on a low-average intelligence level. To get some insight into their mental processes underlying calendar calculation, we first asked whether the identification of dates that were more remote from the current one (i.e. the year of testing) would take longer to work out than those nearer to the current year. Second, we wondered whether identification of dates lying in the future, which were therefore less likely ever to have been practised, would be more difficult, and thus take more time than was needed for dates in the past. Finally, we predicted that date calculation in the current year would be accomplished more quickly than for either past or future years. We asked our participants questions such as 'On what day fell 15 February 1983?' (this was the year of testing) or 'What day was 2 September 1963' or '…20 July 1986?' All dates were within the then current century and the years into which the tested dates fell were 1963, 1973, 1983 (the year of testing), 1986 and 1993.

We noted three aspects of the results. First, the dates in the current year took much less time to identify than those for years in the past or future, and the participants could almost instantly tell the weekdays for dates in that year. Second, for the past and the future, calculation times increased with an increase of the time gap between the present and past or future years. Finally, though the time gaps from the year of testing were shorter for the future (i.e. three and ten years) than for the past (10 and 20 years), the less remote future years needed as much time to calculate as those in the more remote past. Thus though all dates in the current century were in the calculating span of the participants, future years seemed to require longer calculation times.

We concluded from these findings that, because of the familiarity with the current calendar, probably little or no calculation was needed to identify dates in the present year. Most of the savants seemed to have direct access to day/date pairings in the current calendar year. They really 'just knew' the days on which dates in that year fell, and could retrieve these quickly from memory. The faster speeds for nearer than more remote dates might have indicated a backward search in the memory store, starting with the present and going increasingly backwards or further forwards in time. Alternatively, more extensive calculation was needed for them. But perhaps the most interesting result was that though the past dates reached further back than the future ones reached forward, nevertheless calculation of dates 20 years into the past needed approximately the same amount of time as was required for only ten years in the future. This we took as an indication that the longer time needed to identify future dates was that they were much less likely ever to have been practised and memorised. They had to be calculated on the spot. As the savants could do this, it seems that familiarity and practice can only be one of the contributing factors in savant calendar calculation ability, and that other processes must also be operating.

The structure of the calendar has made it possible to devise various formulas, algorithms, tables, perpetual calendars and, more recently, computer programs that allow the user to identify quickly the past and future weekdays of dates. The methods of determining this are usually detailed and quite complex, and can be found in encyclopaedias and almanacs. But there is general consensus among researchers in this area that for two main reasons the savant skill of calendar calculation is unlikely to be based on the use of such published methods. First, it seems improbable that the majority of these individuals, who were all mentally handicapped and at that time lived in institutions, would have had access to the relevant publications concerning these methods. Second, and more important, the mastery of such formulas requires a level of reading, comprehension, learning and numerical ability which is beyond that of most, though not all, savants. As we will see further on, some few savants have indeed a quite outstanding numerical ability, but most have only very basic arithmetical skills. However, in the course of the study I have described, some observations had suggested to us that rules of calendar structure might play a role in savant calendar calculation. Two of the calculators, one of whom had the highest and the other the lowest IQ of the group, had spontaneously said at one point 'April first and July first on the same day' and 'twenty-eight years repeat'. It appeared that the awareness of these rules did not depend on the intelligence level of the participant.

It is regularities and correspondence that make the calendar a structured, repetitive device. One of these is that the calendar structure repeats itself exactly every 28 and every 400 years. Thus if in a particular year a specific date fell on a Monday, after 28 years the same date will fall on the Monday again. Furthermore, certain pairs of months within the same year share the same calendar pattern. March and November are one such identical pair, and so are April and July as well as September and December, and of course in non-leap years February and March. So if in a particular year 11 March is a Tuesday, then 11 November in that year will also be a Tuesday.

We had already demonstrated that it took longer for savants to calculate a more remote date than a less remote one and that future dates took longer to identify than those in the past. In the next study we asked whether dates in years that lay 28 years in the past or future would still take longer to calculate than less distant ones. Alternatively, if the 28-year rule was used, calculation time might be shorter for years divided by a 28-year gap than for less remote years. Thus as the year of testing was now 1984, 28 years in the future would make this the year 2012 and 28 years into the past would make it 1956. The other dates in years we tested were nearer to 1984, i.e. 2002 for the future and 1966 for the past.

We found that the 28-year gap between identical years did not affect calculation times for the past. Thus dates in 1956 took longer to calculate than those in 1966. This is the same kind of result that we got in the previous study. At least over a limited period of time, it appears to be the case that there is either a backward memory search for past dates, and the more remote these dates, the longer the search takes, or more time is needed for their calculations. But a different pattern of results was obtained for future date calculation. Apparently such dates were not stored in memory, but had to be worked out. This took quite a while for dates in the year 2002. But for dates in the year 2012 lying even further in the future (i.e. 28 years) date identification took the same short time as was needed for the current year of testing. The structural identity of these two years resulted in response times that were three times faster than those for the more adjacent future year. We concluded from this that although most of the savants could not tell us about this calendar regularity, they had nevertheless used it for future date calculation.

Next, we set out to test whether the savants would utilise the fact that in certain pairs of months the same weekdays will fall on identical dates. As I have said, such month pairs are March and November, April and July, September and December. We consequently asked for calculation in these corresponding months and compared the time needed to calculate the day for the second member of a date pair with the first, that is, 6 November after it had been identified with the time needed for giving the day of 6 March. The same comparisons were made for the time needed for identification of the second member of a non-identical pair of months, for instance, 14 August following the calculation of 14 October. All dates fell into the current year of testing.

Our results showed that there was a significant gain in speed for naming the day of the second member of a date pair in an identically structured month. However, for non-identically structured months, the second member of a date pair took longer to name than the first. It appears from these results that first a mental check about month identity was carried out. If this confirmed the knowledge that the structure of the two months was the same, the weekday of the second member of the date pair could be given immediately. However, when it was decided that the months' structures differed, separate calculations had to be made for each date in a pair. The conclusion is that the speed in those trials where responses could be predicted on the basis of a calendar rule was faster than in those to which such a rule did not apply.

For the next experiment we used a more complex calendar pattern. In 1986, 1 January was a Wednesday. In the following year this date fell on a Thursday, and in the preceding one on a Tuesday. This pattern, that the first day of any succeeding year moves one day forward and the first day in the preceding moves one day back, only holds when no leap years are involved. We aimed to investigate whether our savants were aware of this moving pattern. We showed them a card, which we also read out to them. On this the seven days of the week were printed out four times, one beneath the other.

We then said to each participant: 'Look at this card. We will pretend that there are no leap years. If this were true, on what day would the next year (year 5) start?' and 'On which day fell the beginning of the year before that shown on the top row?'

This proved to be a difficult problem for the savants and only four of the eight participants solved it successfully. It is of interest that these successful participants all fell into the upper half of the group's intelligent range with IQs between 88 and 56. The four who could not cope with this task all had IQs below 50, and their mental development was at best equivalent to that of a normal seven and a half-year-old child. Thus we have to ask ourselves what had made this present problem more difficult than the two previous ones, which had dealt with making use of the identical structure of certain years and months. As pointed out earlier, years that are 28 years apart share the same pattern, as do the month pairs listed earlier. In the previous studies we made use of this so that the same dates in identical pairs of months, or dates in years that were 28 years apart, always fell on the same days of the week. In contrast, here one had to deduce a 'moving pattern', though this movement was lawful. Nevertheless, this was a problem for the less intelligent savants. In addition to the relevance of IQ, the characteristics of autism may also have played a part in making this task more difficult. As I have suggested, the very features of a rigid, repetitive, predictable calendar structure may 'tune in' with the autistic tendency for just such behavioural patterns, and autistic people, unless they are reasonably bright, may lack the necessary flexibility for inferring a changing structural rule. But having said this, one must take into account that those savants who could not master this task could nevertheless calendar calculate as well as those who did. Without underlying implicit knowledge of these shifts from year to year, calendar calculation could not be accurate. There must thus have been a difference for those autistic savants between implicit knowledge used for their calendar calculation process and another within the context of a specific task demand that lay outside this particular activity.

In a final study of calendar calculators with Neil O'Connor, we returned to our initial hypothesis that this ability was not solely the result of prolonged extensive practice aimed at improving performances. As mentioned, some influential psychologists hold that there is no necessity at all to assume the existence of inherent predispositions and domain-specific potential (i.e. a talent). As I have said, for such a talent to result in high achievement, continuous hard work, as well as the motivation for such application over a long period of time, is necessary. But practice alone will not do, certainly not for savants.

We had come across two children who were both ten years old, and who appeared to show similar calendar calculating abilities to those of the older savants we had tested. The first of these children had been diagnosed as being autistic. His mother had had rubella during the early period of pregnancy, which may have resulted in the child suffering from some congenital brain dysfunction. He began to talk only when aged four and a half years, but at the same time he showed a particularly strong interest in numbers and arithmetic. He had a non-verbal IQ of 90, which is in the low-average range, but his verbal ability was well below that shown on these visuospatial tests. He attended a special school for mentally handicapped children, as he had not been able to cope with mainstream education. However, we found that his numerical abilities were exceptional. When we first realised this, we explained to him the rationale and principles of square root calculation, which were unknown to him at this time. Following this, he immediately proceeded to solve a number of square root problems quickly and accurately.

The second boy had the same age and IQ pattern as the first. Although he attended a mainstream school, he was reported to be inattentive, easily distracted and disruptive, as well as showing some typically autistic features of behaviour. He had no friends and did not play with other children. Although no clinical diagnosis of autism had been made at the time, he would probably be regarded now as suffering from autistic spectrum disorder. His educational progress was reported as being far below expectation, though he could read. He had an intense interest in calendars, though as with the first boy, reports of his calendar calculation skills were purely anecdotal and neither child's ability in this respect had ever been formally assessed.

We tested these two boys repeatedly over a period of one and a half years, to establish whether they would differ from the previously tested savant group, and whether or not they would show any improvement in their performance over the 18-month period. Of course, they may both have practised calculating dates before we began this study, but at least it seemed unlikely that because of their age this would have been very systematic or have occurred over an extended time period.

We first asked each of them to identify days of the week for dates in the current year. We also presented them with dates in years ten and 28 years in the past, as well as with dates that lay ten and 28 years in the future. Both children were fastest in identifying dates in the current year, but the child with a firm diagnosis of autism needed far less time for doing this than the other boy. Like the previously tested older participants, he took only 2.7 seconds for this, compared with 7.2 seconds required by the other boy. The overall response patterns were also different for these two children. The autistic boy's response speed was very fast throughout, but there were no significant effects of either prolongation of time gap or of the 28-year identity rule. Indeed, he was faster than most of the adults who had previously participated, taking on average just over three seconds for all given dates. Consequently, there may not have been much room for further improvement. His arithmetical ability may have been so high that it made any facilitating rule application unnecessary, though it might of course have also been the case that he was not aware of the rule. Like most of our older calculators, he could not give any verbal account in this respect.

In contrast, the second boy was slower in identifying the dates, though his performance, like that of the first participant, was errorless. He was also fastest with date calculation in the year of testing, with an average speed of seven seconds, which is longer than needed by any of the adults. His other responses were also slow, but interestingly he needed only ten seconds to identify dates that lay 28 years in the future, in contrast with an average 19 seconds, nearly twice as long, for dates in those years only ten years in the future. So it appears that though being overall less efficient, he seems to have made use of the 28-year identity rule. There was no improvement over time (i.e. no practice effect) for either child.

At the outset of this series of studies we had asked the question whether savant calendar calculators extracted and used the rules and regularities of calendar structure in their calculation process. Prior to these experiments visual imagery and rote memory (i.e. knowledge through repetition), and more recently continuous goal-directed practice, had been held to be the main determinants of such an astounding savant ability. The result of our investigations led us to conclude that other strategies in addition to, or instead of, those listed above must be involved. Irrespective of their IQ levels, our participants used rule-based strategies for most of the tasks set for them, although some failed to discover such rules for the most inferential problem. But they were all proficient calendar calculators, and this was so in spite of their varying intelligence levels as well as their differing arithmetical skills. As early as 1907, Mitchell had concluded about great numerical calculators that some such people simply used the properties of numbers, others brought arithmetical procedures to bear and others again discovered ingenious shortcuts and symmetries which they used. However, these different strategies did not appear to affect their performance levels. As in such normal talented people, individual differences in mental processing strategies will also apply to savants. This must not be overlooked when we seek to understand the nature of their high-level specific abilities.

In the next chapter further variables that contribute to savant calendar calculating ability will be investigated. Here, I like to remind you again that our calendar still gives us a far from completely accurate account of the passage of time. All our advances in this respect have not yet managed to dismiss the observation of Roger Bacon, who was a distinguished original thinker and scientist in the Middle Ages. Duncan quoted him as writing in 1267:

> *The calendar is intolerable to all wisdom,*
> *The horror of all astronomy,*
> *And the laughing stock from a mathematician point of view.*

In spite of the remaining truth of this statement, to have deduced some of the rules, structures and predictable calendar patterns, and to have used these in date identification, has to be regarded as a considerable feat for people with autism, as well as limited general intelligence and reasoning capacity.

7

Date Memory

'When did Aunt Hilda visit us last?' 'On 2 October 1987, and that was a Friday.' 'When did I take you last to see the dentist?' 'On Wednesday 3 July 1996.' Such precise information is frequently obtained from children who subsequently become savant calendar calculators. Most of us do not remember the dates of such events, and sometimes we may even have forgotten those that have some significance for us, such as the birthday of a close friend or even the date of our own wedding anniversary. But for calendar calculators such dates had become very significant long before they began their own calendar calculations. Until recently the reports of this outstanding date memory had tended to be purely anecdotal. We thought it would be worthwhile to investigate the nature of this memory and the role it played in savant calendar calculation. Therefore our research associate Lisa Heavey, in co-operation with Linda Pring and me, attempted to tackle this issue.

First, we needed to establish whether savant date memory was really superior to that of individuals who are not able to calendar calculate. Even if the savants were better able to remember calendar information than other individuals, would this be a consequence of a generally better memory for all sorts of things? What is the role of memory in the calendar calculation process? Are savants able to calculate dates because they remember them, or do they remember dates because they can calendar calculate? O'Connor and I had been able to show that they used features of calendar structure in their date calculation. Were such features also stored in their memories? Before going on to address these questions, it may be useful to consider briefly how memory generally functions.

What is best retained in memory tends not to be a collection of separate, unrelated items. Instead, how well we remember something usually depends on the degree to which we can organise it, and how well new information can be connected to other related knowledge. But of course we can also remember series of items that have little meaning but are recalled after practice and repetition (e.g. telephone numbers), and we do not even need practice if we can make out that some series of items are governed by a particular rule. Thus, having to recall a long series of numbers, such as 5, 8, 12, 15, 19, 22, 26, etc., needs no practice at all once we have been told, or have found out ourselves, that the rule that governs this series is adding alternately 3 and 4 for the next number. All that we then have to do is to apply this rule and we can go on for as long as we like. Such an organised and rule-governed memory may be relevant for savant calendar information; as I have already mentioned, 'benchmarks' (i.e. the memory for single significant dated events) might also play a part in this remarkable skill.

What notably distinguished Lisa Heavey's memory studies was that the savant participants were for the most part not required to carry out calendar calculations at all. All that they were asked to do was to remember lists of dates that had been shown and read out to them before. In some of the studies this approach made it possible to compare date memory by calendar calculators with that of other participants without this ability. It also allowed one to explore in some detail the underlying knowledge on which calendar calculations were based. Prior to these investigations, Neil O'Connor and I had already shown that other savants' superior memory was restricted to the area of their specific ability. We had tested a group of individuals with mental impairments who could recall details about all London bus routes, giving precise information about their numbers, stops and final destination. They also knew in which garage each bus was housed overnight. We presented them, as well-matched comparison individuals, with ten different verbal, numerical and visuospatial memory tasks that were taken from various intelligence test batteries. There we found no differences in the general memory ability between these two groups. On the other hand, the savants were much superior in recalling lists of bus numbers.

In Lisa Heavey's first study, eight calendar calculators took part. All of them could calculate dates between 1900 and 2000, and quite a few of them could do this over a much longer time period. Their verbal intelligence test scores ranged from an IQ of 40 to 80, with a group average IQ of 65. All except one participant had been diagnosed as suffering from autism. Other individuals with the same diagnoses, intelligence levels and ages as the savants were used as comparison participants. In a preliminary investigation the experimenter simply read out a series of ten words or numbers in random order, and each participant was required to repeat these straight back. For instance, she would say '7...5...3...2...4... (etc.)' or 'house...knife... box...chair... (etc.)' and the participant had to repeat these in the same order. It was found that the immediate memory spans of the two groups of individuals did not differ, but all were able to recall more numbers than words. The reason for this might be that there are after all only ten digits (we did not use 0, but only 1 to 10) but there are any number of words from which to choose. On average, between five and six numbers and between four and five words were correctly recalled. The results from the finding of this first experiment extended the earlier cited findings obtained by O'Connor and myself with those savants who knew all about London buses. Taken together they suggest that a generally superior immediate memory does not appear to be a decisive factor for savant ability.

It was examined next how well the savants could remember information after a somewhat longer interval between the presentation of the material and the requirement to recall it. This represented a more difficult test of memory as the participants were asked to chat with the experimenter during the interval, which prevented them from being able silently to rehearse the items to be recalled. Lists of differently dated years such as 1922, 1846, 2089, 1754, etc. were read out, and after two minutes of conversation the savants were significantly better able to recall this calendar-related information than the controls. In addition, the two groups had also been tested for their memory of single-word strings (e.g. hand, path, salt) as a measure of general, non-calendrical memory. With such words the savants were found not to be superior to controls in their memory capacity. These results confirmed that any memory advantage observed in the savant group was confined to information that was related to the calendar.

As stated, all the savant participants could calculate dates over at least 100 years and most of them could do this over 200 or 300 years. The question asked in the next study was whether savants would better remember those dated years that were within their calculation span than those years that were not. It was found that the best memory scores were obtained for years dated in the twentieth century, in which all savants could calculate. Those in the twenty-first and nineteenth centuries were the next best recalled and these centuries were still in the time spans over which most of the participants calculated. For these time spans the calculating savants could remember significantly more dates than the control participants. However, as their memory for seventeenth-century years was in fact not much better than that of the control group members, there appeared to be a relationship between memory for dates and the ability to calendar calculate.

This apparent relationship between calendar calculation and the memory for dated years was the subject of the next investigation. As this involved actual date calculation no control participants could be included here. Remembering was tested in two different conditions: the first only required recall of a list of dates that had been read out by the savants; the second required them to calculate the weekdays for dates in the list. Thus in the 'study condition' the savant calculators were successively shown and read aloud 18 different dates such as 'Monday 7 January 1980'. Following this, the whole list of dates could be inspected for a further 15 seconds. It was stressed that one should look carefully at all the items and think about them.

In the second, the 'calculating condition', the same individuals were again told that they would be shown 18 dates (of course different ones from those studied). This time though the weekday was omitted from the dates, as for instance in '24 January 1927', and each participant was asked to tell the experimenter the day of the week for each given date. No mention of trying to remember the dates was made in either condition, and half of the individuals first studied and then calculated while the reverse was true for the rest. After the completion of 'study' or 'calculation', the experimenter chatted for about five minutes with each individual. Then, for each condition, a surprise memory test was given in which lists of ten dates (without weekdays) were presented, five of which had been shown previously while five were new 'distractor' dates. The participants had to point out those dates which they had been shown previously. It was found that significantly more of the calculated dates were correctly recognised than those that had only been studied. Thus it seems not to be so much the mere exposure to date information, rather actively doing something with it, that enhances date memory. I will return to this conclusion in the context of other savant abilities.

The next series of Lisa Heavey's studies concentrated on exploring the format in which calendar knowledge is stored. You will recall that the calendar is a highly structured device which follows strict rules and regularities. Is the memory of calendar calculators therefore organised to reflect such calendar structure? No control participants took part here, as this experiment was aimed to investigate possible differences *within* the savant group that were due to the nature of the information to be retained. One of the basic building blocks of calendar structure is the regularity of weekday occurrence. Every eighth day will fall on the same day of the week. If one knows that 1 May 1995 was a Monday this allows one to infer that 8, 15, 22 and 29 May were also Mondays. A knowledge about the number of days in every month will in addition enable one to work out every Monday in the whole year. This illustrates how the realisation of such regularities, even if it remains implicit, might lead to successful calendar calculation. Therefore the following study on savant date memory compared the memory of dates that share the same day of the week with others that do not.

Each savant was shown two different types of date lists for which his memory was subsequently tested. In one of these, eight dates in a particular year (for instance, 1991) all fell on the same weekday, but of course weekdays were not included in the list. It simply consisted of such dates as 10 October 1991, 27 June 1991, 7 March 1991, etc. In contrast, in the second type of list, taken from a different year, the presented eight dates all fell on different weekdays. Such a list consisted of dates such as 11 July 1989 (Tuesday), 4 March 1989 (Saturday), 20 December 1989 (Wednesday) etc., but again as in the other list the actual weekdays, given here in brackets, were not shown.

Each single date was exposed for five seconds and read out by the participant together with the experimenter. The savants were asked to try to remember these dates. Following this, the whole list was shown again for ten seconds, and after one minute's interval filled with conversation, each individual was asked to recall as many of the dates as possible. It was found that the savants remembered an average of six dates that had been contained in the same weekday lists, but only an average of four dates of different day lists. Statistical tests confirmed that there was a highly significant difference between the recall of the two list types. Every single savant remembered more dates from the 'same day' than the 'different day' ones.

After memory testing had been concluded, both the same and the different weekday lists of eight dates were shown again, and each savant was asked whether he noticed anything particular about them. The two participants with the highest IQs (80 and 79) could give an account of the relationship between dates in the 'same day' list. The others gave no indication of such an awareness, even after repeated questioning. However, in spite of this lack of a verbal accounting by the majority, all had shown an effect on memory of dates falling on the same day of the week. This indicates an underlying knowledge base of calendar structure, although such knowledge need not be consciously formulated.

The next study referred back to my previous finding with O'Connor that the repetition of the calendar structure every 28 years had facilitated savants' calculation. As stated, every 28 years the same date in the calendar will fall on the same day of the week. In this experiment it was attempted to contrast the savants' memory for dates linked according to this calendar regularity with those years which did not conform to such a regular calendar feature. Eight dates from each of two different lists had to be recalled. In one of these the interval between the dates was 28 years and in the second the yearly interval was 23 years. Of course the dates in the 28-year interval list all fell on the same weekday, and those on the control list did not. However, no weekdays were presented in either of the lists, only years and dates were given. Each date was shown and read out; after this, each complete list of eight dates was again inspected by the participant. Following a brief chat, every savant was then asked to recall as many dates from each of the two lists as he remembered, but identification of the days on which the dates fell was not required.

It was found that from the 28-year list a minimum of six of the eight given dates was recalled. Four of the eight participants retained all eight dates. From the other list, on average only four dates were remembered, with none of the participants recalling all eight dates. The lowest recall score on this list was one date and the highest was five. The same two savants who previously had given a verbal account of the relationship between dates, could also state what differentiated the 28-year dates from the others. But as before, the inability by the majority to state the relationship between years did not prevent them from using the structural regularity within the calendar to aid their recall. Thus, while the previous experiment had demonstrated the effect on memory of weekday regularities, it was concluded that this study had succeeded in revealing enhanced memory for dates organised in accordance with a structural feature of the calendar about year identity.

Lisa Heavey's following investigation about remembering structural calendar features was concerned with leap years and their significance for calendar memory. As mentioned before, when Julius Caesar introduced his calendar reorganisation to bring the year to 365 days, this consisted of alternating 30- and 31-day months. The exception to this was February, which at that time had 29 days, except 30 days in a leap year. Though this made the Roman calendar the most accurate in the world, it still led to errors and periodical drifts. Therefore, a further correction was subsequently made, resulting in February having 28 days, except at every fourth year when a 29th day was added. The resulting Julian calendar by then approached the solar year quite closely. But even this revision did not deal adequately with the problem of drift. Therefore in the sixteenth century Pope Gregory XIII ordered a commission to deal with this. Their solution was that although normally leap years are omitted in century years (e.g. 1700, 1800, 1900), the year 2000 should contain a 29 February. Thus with commendable foresight the Pope issued a decree on 24 February 1582 that stated: 'ano vero 2000 more consueto dies bissextus intercaletur, Februario dies 29 continente'. He thereby ordered that in the year 2000 February should contain 29 days. Further alterations may have to be made in the future, because in comparison with the solar year our calendar year is still too long by some minutes.

TOURO COLLEGE LIBRARY

Leap years have to be included in the knowledge base that underlies calendar calculation, otherwise day–date identification will not be accurate. These years represent structurally anomalous features recurring at regular intervals. For the present study, two lists were shown and read out to each of the previously tested savants. One consisted of eight leap years from the twentieth century, though these were not presented in chronological order, so that 1960 was followed by 1944, 1988, 1976, and so on. The years in the other list were non-leap years – 1978, 1917, 1966, 1953, etc. Sure enough, when asked to recall each list, the savants remembered five leap year dates, but only three dates of the non-leap years were recalled on average, resulting in a statistically significant difference between the memorability of the lists. This is further confirmation that regular calendar features affect savant date memory.

Thus far, this series of memory studies has been concerned with the effect of calendar structure on savant date memory. Yet perhaps the most convincing demonstration that savant calendar calculation does rely on a knowledge system of rules and regularities which interconnect different dates into a network is provided by Lisa Heavey's next experiment – an investigation of memory for Easter Sundays. Easter is an event which is not determined by structural calendar regularities, but instead it is a 'movable feast'. It has largely been forgotten that at the Last Supper Jesus and his disciples celebrated the beginning of the week of Passover, which commemorates the exodus of the Jews from Egypt under Moses' leadership. The date of the resurrection of Christ on the following Sunday after his crucifixion on Good Friday is therefore determined by the Jewish moon-governed calendar year. The time the moon takes to go through its phases does not correspond to the earth's calendar months. Therefore Easter Day drifts in our present solar calendar. The key point is that unlike the relationships between dates in the lists of the previous studies, Easter is a date which is not determined by our calendar's structure.

TOURO COLLEGE LIBRARY

The study compared memory for Easter Sunday dates and non-Easter Sundays in different years within the twentieth century. The same group of eight savants who had participated in the previous set of investigations took part in this one. They were asked to recall two different lists of eight Sunday dates. One contained Easter Sunday dates and the second consisted of other non-Easter dates, each also falling on a Sunday. Dates from both lists were taken from March and April. The participants were told only that they would see two lists of dates that all fell on Sundays. Following the presentation of each list, they were asked to recall as many of its dates as possible. Alternate individuals had been shown the Easter dates first and the others the non-Easter dates. As predicted, the savants' memory for the two lists did not differ. They remembered on average five dates of the Easter Sundays and five non-Easter Sunday dates. When questioned whether they had noticed any-thing special about the dates, only the savant who had also been able to verbalise previous list characteristics, pointed to the appro-priate one and stated 'they are all Easter'. He was also the only one who showed a marked difference in recalling the dates of the two lists, remembering seven Easter but only four non-Easter Sundays. For the other savants, because Easter is not an intrinsic feature of calendar structure, but is event related, the Easter dates would not reflect the format in which savant calendar knowledge is stored in memory.

An analogy here might be useful for the reader. Non-structural date knowledge is independent of what one might call the 'grammar' of the calendar. If one would take the language system as being loosely analogous to such a distinction between single events and rule-governed structures, one might assume that events act like words. Single events are something like a calendrical vocabulary. In language a word is an arbitrary label and one has to learn that this animal is called a dog and that flower is a tulip. Each word has its own specific meaning, not unlike a specific dated event. But vocab-ularies differ from grammar, as has been pointed out previously.

Children acquiring the grammar of their native language can extrapolate from sentences they have heard to produce spontaneous new sentences. The example I gave was that in English there is word order of subject–verb–object. Once a child has grasped the meaning of 'I want this', an inherent genetic switch mechanism will be set and the child uses the same structure when producing 'I eat this' or 'I try this'. If one were to compare such a process with that of calendar calculation, such an analogue must of course be qualified by the fact that acquisition of calendar structure, unlike that of grammar, is not an inherent feature of development. But we might nevertheless regard event-related knowledge as giving particular meanings to dates, as words convey specific meaning to things. Calendar structure on the other hand might be regarded as a 'calendrical grammar' that is governed by rules and regularities. Once they are realised, these rules can be extrapolated to enable one to produce, like new sentences, new day–date relations, but the dates for Easter do not form part of such a 'calendrical grammar'.

What then does the study of date memory tell us about how savant calendar knowledge develops? The beginning of the process might be that examples of day–date pairings are gained through a range of personally significant events, such as trips to the seaside, visits from relatives and birthdays. An interest in such information, which is expressed early in life by many calendar calculators, will provide continuous examples of this kind. Through constant exposure, the savants will extract a knowledge of the sequential daily and weekly structure of the calendar, i.e. 1st is a Monday, 2nd is a Tuesday, 3rd is a Wednesday, etc. Thus he is beginning to associate the sequence of days with dates in the format of a seven-day repetition, though this need not be a conscious process. Eventually such implicit knowledge will begin to span weeks, i.e. if 1st is a Monday, then 8th, 15th, etc. are also Mondays. This in turn will gradually extend across months, so that if 30th is a Sunday in a 30-day month, then 7th is also a Sunday in the following month. In effect the calendar calculators are simply learning new numerical sequences (i.e. 1–7, 1–30, 1–31, 1–28), and the Monday to Sunday series is mapped onto this. Constant exposure to such sequencing will re-emphasise the regularities of calendar structure, such as which two months within any non-leap year share the same pattern of day–date pairing (i.e. begin on the same weekday). As mentioned, March and November and April and July are two such month pairs, so that if 1 March is a Monday then 1 November will also be a Monday, and as I have already pointed out the savants make use of such knowledge in day–date identification.

For the structure of the following year all one needs to know is the day on which it starts (i.e. the weekday of 1 January). This will shift forward by one day each year, so if it is a Monday in the current year, it will be a Tuesday in the next. In fact there are only 14 possible yearly configurations of day–date relations, seven of them referring to non-leap and the other seven to leap years. The savant knowing this has only to work out the day on which the next year starts. I must stress again that by using the term 'knowing' here I do not necessarily mean to convey a conscious knowledge that can be verbally stated. Rather it can be compared to knowing the syntactical rules of one's own language and using these correctly without necessarily being able to state them. But just as some people can verbalise rules of grammar, so some savants can tell us the calendar rules. As the calendar is a uniquely closed system with fixed relationships between individual components and a limited number of rules, it is not surprising that it appeals to individuals with autism. They take great pleasure in their ability to predict events in such a static, orderly system.

As will become clear further on, the same processing strategy as that on which calendar calculation is based is also apparent in other domains of savant talent. Savant ability appears to take a route leading from the detail to the whole, thereby reversing our dominant tendency of information processing. As was pointed out earlier, this begins with wholistic perception and memory, from which probable details are subsequently reconstructed. But as is shown by the block design test, on which those with autism tend to do particularly well, they can not only segment a total configuration, but are also able to reconstruct the wholistic pattern from such segments. Such a reconstruction process of individual fragments into coherent patterns seems to underlie the development of potential savant abilities. For calendar calculating savants, their initial interest in single dates prompts them to obtain such information continuously. This would facilitate a gradual process of combining these single elements in an interconnected knowledge base mirroring calendar structure. It would eventually enable the calendar calculator not only to calculate dates in the past, but also to generate new future ones for which calendar information had not been available and which could not have been practised and remembered. 'The distinction between past, present and future is only an illusion,' wrote Albert Einstein. Not so for calendar calculators! For them, these distinctions have a meaningful and tangible reality.

8

Numbers

The first indication of prehistoric quasi-mathematical awareness comes from regular, repetitive patterns on pots and cave walls. Using numbers probably started with indicating precise quantities through the use of the ten digits of the two hands. Indeed in English the term 'digit' is still used as a synonym for a finger as well as a number. Simon Singh has given us a lucid exposition of the history of mathematics in *Fermat's Last Theorem*. The first notational number accounts came, as so much else of civilisation, from Babylon and Egypt and originated at about the same time as script. Egyptian records from 1800 BC provide evidence that by then decimals and fractions were used, and the Babylonians at this time had tables for multiplication and division as well as for roots and squares. These Mesopotamian civilisations used their mathematical knowledge purely for practical purposes, such as distribution of goods, trade, and superb architecture through the application of sophisticated geometry. It was left to the Greeks, with their interest in philosophy and logic, to develop the notion of mathematical proof towards the beginning of the sixth century BC. Mathematics for its own sake in an abstract form was initiated by the philosophers Thales and Pythagoras, the latter stating that it was necessary to study numbers in order to understand the world.

The numerical operations of addition, subtraction and multiplication are of course rather straightforward. The result of such calculations with whole numbers is always another whole number. But there are aspects of division which make this particular operation somewhat more complicated. This is because there are some numbers that are not divisible without a remainder except by 1 or by themselves. These are called 'prime numbers', and for instance 2, 3, 5, 7, 11, 13, 17, 19, 23 and 29 are such primes. Towards the end of the first century BC, the Greek mathematician Euclid provided the first mathematical proof that there is an infinite number of them. There is no largest prime number. But from Euclid's time till today people have tried in vain to discover an underlying pattern that would predict their occurrence. Perhaps there is no pattern and prime-number distribution is inherently random.

Eventually, through the Greeks and the Romans, mathematical knowledge spread to India and the Islamic world. There it was further developed and the term 'algorithm' (the process of applying a rule) is in fact derived from the name of the Muslim algebraic scholar al-Khwarizmi. The Arab way of writing numbers, which is still used today, represented a considerable improvement on the rather cumbersome Roman numerical notation. The development of Eastern number theory eventually found its way back to the West via the Arab presence in Spain and the translation of Arabic and Greek mathematical texts, which led to renewed interest in this topic in Europe during the Middle Ages. However, it was during the time of the Renaissance and the period following that modern algebra really took off in Europe, culminating in the mathematical geniuses Isaac Newton and Pierre de Fermat.

In the seventeenth century, Fermat is reported to have provided the first prime-number theorem. However, though the facts he stated have remained indisputable, the theorem itself unfortunately was lost. Theorems not only account for observable instances of a phenomenon, but provide absolute proof for all such possible instances. Fermat provided proof that all prime numbers had to fall into one of two categories. The first type of prime always equals the sum of $4 \times n + 1$ (where n is some particular number). The second category contains all those primes that result from $4 \times n - 1$. So the prime number 13 equals $4 \times 3 + 1$, while 19 equals $4 \times 5 - 1$. This formula holds for all primes. Simple, isn't it? But it took the eighteenth century's great Swiss mathematician Leonhard Euler seven years of work to rediscover the proof of Fermat's prime-number theorem.

One fact about prime numbers still evades mathematical proof. Christian Goldbach had written in 1724 that any even number larger than 24 can be represented as a sum of two primes. Thus 26 is $13 + 13$, 72 is $19 + 53$, and so on. Computers have confirmed this fact for all even numbers up to 400 billion, but to date nobody has been able to prove it mathematically.

This chapter reports investigations designed to explain how an autistic savant, who had an extraordinary arithmetical ability, was able to identify and generate prime numbers. Outstanding arithmetical abilities by otherwise mentally impaired individuals have been reported since the eighteenth century. One such early account tells about a mentally retarded man who, when 80 years old, could still quickly answer questions such as how many seconds a man had lived when aged 70 years, 17 days and 12 hours. The correct answer he gave was 2,210,500,800 seconds and this mentally impaired individual had taken leap years into account for his calculation. There are several reports of idiots savants who could mentally add columns of six-digit figures, and others who were able to multiply and divide large numbers within seconds.

Savant arithmetical calculators often show a fascination for numbers at a very early age, counting things continuously; consequently they become familiar with number sequences. This then leads them gradually to grouping and extracting inter-numerical relationships, although these are hardly ever explicitly stated and become evident only in such an individual's increasing calculation skills. Between great mental calculators without any cognitive impairments there are marked individual differences in the strategies employed. Some individuals do have an outstanding numerical memory, while others do not. Some use shortcuts and near guesses, others detailed rapid calculation. All are able to deal instantly with numerical constituents of any number they come across, as vividly illustrated by a remark of that great mental calculator Wim Klein. 'Numbers are friends to me,' he said, 'it doesn't mean the same to you, does it, 3844? For you it is just a 3 and an 8 and a 4 and a 4. But I say "Hi 62 squared!"' Of the Swiss mathematical genius Euler it was said that he 'calculated without apparent effort, as men breathe or as eagles sustain themselves in the air'.

Of course, savant numerical calculators are not geniuses; but though their ability is on a much lower level, it nevertheless far exceeds that of most of the rest of us. And savants do seem to share with the great calculators the effortless appreciation of the nature of numbers. The brilliant writer and neurologist, Oliver Sacks, observing a famous pair of savant twins first described by W.A. Horwitz, watched them playing a game where they rapidly alternated in calling our successive prime numbers of up to 20 digits. These twins had a general mental capacity equal to that of a nine to ten year old, and it is certainly the case that an outstanding memory for numbers has been reported in nearly every case of savant mental calculation. Sacks reported that the twins could recall numbers of up to 300 digits. But such formidable memory is not confined to savants. For instance, the great twentieth-century mathematician Aitkin, who was also a formidable mental calculator, dictated up to 100 decimal places after a number to his secretary without a script and then repeated these after a while to verify whether she had written them down correctly. It has been experimentally demonstrated that deliberate continuous practice by people who are not particularly gifted for arithmetic can considerably improve their numerical and calendrical memory. But of course this does not necessarily imply that such a route to high achievement is the same as that leading to outstanding attainment by those with inherent interests in and talents for the numerical domain.

Most savant arithmetical calculators are diagnosed as suffering from autism or Asperger Syndrome, and the majority can also calendar calculate. As mentioned, autistic individuals have a tendency to segment information, and the decomposing of whole numbers into their constituent elements might thus suit their cognitive processing style.

Neil O'Connor and I came to know Michael when he participated in the calendar calculation studies which I have already described (Chapter 6). He was then 20 years old. When aged three, he had been diagnosed as showing all the symptoms of classical autism as described by Kanner. At the age of ten months he had convulsions, and these occurred again between the ages of two and three years. He has never shown any responsiveness to people, reacting to neither speech nor gestures. He did not look at things when someone pointed at them, never waved goodbye or responded to cuddling. Michael is not deaf, but he seemed not to understand any language at all and did not himself develop any speech. Yet, aged three, he could assemble jigsaw puzzles of 100 pieces and as for many autistic children it did not make any difference to him whether he could see what was pictured or whether the pieces were blank. He has remained entirely without language, and though he was taught some sign language gestures he never used these spontaneously. But he was able mentally to add, subtract, multiply and divide large numbers when they were written down. He could write numbers himself, though these were somewhat hard to read.

We found that he could not cope with an intelligence test in which he is told a word and has to point at the one of four pictures which illustrated it. On a non-verbal social maturity scale his performance level was equivalent to that of a normal ten year old, but when we gave him a non-verbal test of intelligence, we obtained a high IQ of 128. On this test some items represent abstract shapes from which the odd-one-out has to be selected. For instance, three shapes might contain only straight lines, whereas the fourth one also has a curved one. Michael could solve such spatial problems at the very highest level of difficulty. However, for other test items, the odd one out does not belong to the same conceptual class of other pictured objects. For instance, a picture of a piece of furniture might be displayed among those of animals. Michael could only cope with such problems at a very low level, and this discrepancy in dealing with abstract, non-representational, in contrast to meaningful items was reflected in his performance. Indeed, at a more recently given purely visuospatial intelligence test, not requiring semantic reasoning, Michael obtained an IQ of 140, which is very high indeed and near the top end of what can be obtained on such a scale.

Michael now lives in a sheltered community of people with autism, where he has learned to weave and he produces very beautiful and complex patterns. It is of relevance that both his parents have university degrees in mathematics, though neither of them works as a professional mathematician. When we were told of his arithmetical ability in addition to his calendar calculating skill, we asked his mother whether he could recognise and produce prime numbers. She said that she had never tried him on that, and at our request she gave him a list of large numbers to divide, which included some primes. In her letter to us she then wrote: 'When Michael came to these prime numbers, he looked at me as though he thought I was mad.' We thus decided to test the nature of Michael's prime-number ability. A psychologist, who also had a university degree in mathematics, acted as a comparison participant.

In our investigation, in which we aimed at an understanding of Michael's strategy for dealing with prime numbers, we used three tasks, each presented at three levels of difficulty. Because of his inability to deal with language, Michael could not understand any spoken instructions, so we used written numerical examples to show him what to do, which he appeared to grasp instantly. First, we required him and his control participant to factorise numbers. Second, prime numbers had to be identified from among non-primes. Third, primes had to be generated by writing them down.

For factorising, a given number has to be divided successively into its composites until a prime number is reached and no further division is possible. In the early nineteenth century Colburn, a famous mathematical child prodigy, could rapidly factorise any given number containing up to seven digits when he was six years old. However, he was not able to say how he did this, and often started to cry when pestered with persistent questioning. But one night when he was aged eight, he woke up his father saying: 'I can tell you how I find the numbers.' His father immediately wrote down what the child told him, and in fact he had used a theorem for factorising first stated in the third century BC by the Greek mathematician Eratosthenes for the identification of prime numbers. When done in pre-computer days the method was lengthy with large numbers, though of course the little Colburn could use it instantly.

In our first study we presented each of our two participants with numbers from 212 to 221, numbers from 1001 to 1011, and finally numbers from 10002 to 10011. For each of these 30 numbers, we asked them to write down the factors until a prime was reached and no further division was possible. This was done correctly by the control participant with a mathematics degree in eight instances out of ten in the hundreds, seven in the thousands, and four in the ten thousands. Michael recognised that a prime had been reached in nine, eight and three instances for three-, four- and five-digit numbers respectively, and the difference between the two participants is statistically not significant. But Michael was much faster than the control in factorising the numbers, particularly in the hundreds and ten thousands.

Michael's fast responses with the three-digit numbers might have indicated that he had become familiar with these divisions and had practised them before, but this seemed less likely with those numbers in the larger ranges. The overall similar time for four-digit numbers by both participants indicates that they may have used a similar strategy, which resulted in similar calculation speeds. But in the ten thousands Michael's calculation was much faster. It is thus possible that, like normal prodigies, he could apply an appropriate algorithm without having conscious access to it. While his calculation times for four- and five-figure numbers are statistically identical, those of the control participant took significantly more time as number size increased.

The next study was concerned with the recognition of prime numbers. The participants were each given three lists of 30 numbers, one in the hundreds, one in the thousands and one in the ten thousands. Every such list contained ten randomly interspersed primes, which had to be marked. In the hundreds, Michael was very nearly 100 per cent correct, whereas the control participant was only correct with two-thirds of the items. With four-digit numbers, correct identification for both participants was similar – 18 out of 30 numbers for the control, and 22 out of 30 for the savant were correctly identified as either primes or non-primes. With five-digit numbers Michael gave only 15 correct responses out of a possible 30, whereas the control participant identified 23 of the numbers correctly as primes or non-primes.

However, when correctly identifying prime numbers, Michael was very much faster than the participant with the mathematics degree. He needed just over one second for identifying a prime in the hundreds compared with 11.5 seconds required for the control. For the correct recognition of four-digit numbers the savant took less than three seconds, while the other participant needed more than four times as long. The respective amount of time needed for identifying prime numbers in the ten thousands was two seconds for the savant and more than ten seconds for the control.

Michael's identification of prime numbers is thus almost instant. It is not possible to say whether he had initially realised that some numbers cannot be divided and had then stored these in memory, or whether his speed of calculation is very fast and therefore leads to errors with the largest set of numbers. But his prime-number identification speed is comparable to that of normal 'lightning calculators'.

Finally, we asked both participants in this study to generate prime numbers. As previously, written examples were given, which Michael seemed to understand instantly. Each participant was asked to write ten prime numbers in the range from 227 to 281, ten more between 1019 to 1091 and a further ten between 10037 and 10133. Thus, in all, 30 prime numbers had to be generated.

Overall, the control participant wrote down 12 numbers incorrectly as primes, and Michael made 11 such errors. He correctly generated nine out of ten primes in the hundreds range, and five each in the thousands and ten thousands. The results were very similar for the control participant, with eight, five and five correct primes for the respective ranges. As in the other two tasks, Michael was very much faster, needing six, six and ten seconds to generate primes for the increasing digit numbers, while the mathematics graduate needed 13, 26 and 50 seconds respectively. That a similar strategy was used by both participants is suggested by the similarity in their errors. Both tended to mark the same numbers as primes when in fact they were not, and failed to recognise the same prime numbers. The former errors occurred most frequently when numbers were not divisible by either three or eleven. The control participant in fact reported that he had mentally put the numbers into three distinct categories. The first consisted of those that could be divided by 3 or 11, as these were simple divisions. In the second category he included all those numbers which were divisible by divisors other than 3 and 11, and in the third category were primes, i.e. those numbers which could not be divided at all.

Neither participant ever mistakenly thought that numbers which could be divided by 3 or 11 were primes. On the other hand, particularly in the four-digit number range, Michael thought that six numbers were primes when in fact they were not, and the control made four such errors. A similar error pattern was also evident in the factorising and recognition tasks. Thus errors arose through both participants mistakenly identifying those numbers as primes which could not be easily divided, and this contra-indicates that Michael had simply memorised the prime numbers.

During this investigation of prime-number ability, an entertaining incident occurred. One day a large luxurious car drew up in front of our rather dilapidated office building and we saw a liveried chauffeur helping an elderly man up the three narrow, steep flights of stairs to our rooms. Our unexpected visitor was the late Lord Rothschild, who had heard of our work with the savant prime-number calculator. Lord Rothschild had at some time worked for the British Secret Service. There he had got to hear that during the Cold War period the Russians in their coded messages appeared to make use of a system that enabled them to predict prime number occurrences. Although as I have pointed out no one has as yet discovered such a pattern for their occurrence, Lord Rothschild nevertheless wondered whether Michael had some mental representation of such a system. We did not think so, and of course Michael's complete absence of language comprehension made it impossible to question him about it. So Lord Rothschild's question remained unanswered and the Russian code unbroken.

When first publishing our results from the three experiments outlined here, Neil O'Connor and I had proposed that the savant's strategy for prime-number identification seemed similar to that first outlined by the Greek astronomer and mathematician Eratosthenes in the third century BC. Despite the fact that the occurrence of prime numbers does not appear to follow an identifiable pattern and may indeed be inherently random, Eratosthenes had found a method to determine whether given numbers are, or are not, primes. Let us for instance assume that we want to find all the prime numbers below 64. To do this we first identify all those primes that are smaller than the square route of 64 (i.e. 8). Doing this we obtain the numbers 2, 3, 5 and 7. The next step is to eliminate as primes all even numbers and all those which are multiples of the identified primes, as for instance 9, 15, 21, 49, 56, 63, etc. After this process the remaining numbers 11, 13, 17, 19, 23, 29, 31, 37, 41, 43, 47, 53, 59, 61 are all the prime numbers below 64. This procedure is applicable to the identification of all prime numbers. With large numbers the method does of course become cumbersome and lengthy, though, as we have heard, the young Colburn could do it in a flash. He thereby demonstrated that an algorithm such as that of Eratosthenes need not be consciously formulated to be instantly applied. In order to test further whether Michael had indeed used the Eratosthenes paradigm, O'Connor and I, together with our colleague Mike Anderson, carried out more investigations into the strategy he used.

In the first of these, a new control participant took part, who had a degree in mathematics and electronics. He and Michael were again asked to identify prime numbers, this time under more controlled conditions. The numbers they had to deal with fell into three categories: small (below 200), medium (between 200 and 500), and large (above 500). The non-primes were divided into those divisible by 2 or 5 in one set, those that could be divided by 3, 7 or 11 in the second, and the third set contained numbers divisible by 13, 17 or 19. Numbers were shown singly in a random order on a screen, and the participant had to indicate whether or not each was a prime. The time needed for such identification was recorded.

Michael's performance was almost errorless, giving only two incorrect responses in a total of 108 trials. One of these occurred when he thought that a small number was not a prime when in fact it was, and the other when he identified a large non-prime as a prime number. The control participant made 17 errors and in most of these he thought that numbers were primes when in fact they were not.

Michael was not only more often correct, but also much faster than the other individual. On average his responses were given in 14 seconds compared with the other participant's time of 52 seconds. Both took longer to classify the larger numbers, and both needed more time to identify primes than non-primes. Thus their overall response pattern was very similar. Both of them also needed more time when a larger divisor was required. When questioned, the control participant said that in essence he had applied the Eratosthenes strategy, and in view of the similarities between his pattern of results and those of the savant, one can assume that the same was done by Michael.

In order to test this hypothesis an even more rigorous method was used in the next study with Anderson. He devised two computer simulations: one mirrored the Eratosthenes method for identifying primes; and the second assumed that prime numbers were serially stored in memory and identified by searching through the memory store. The data obtained from Michael in the previous study and that of a group of undergraduate mathematics students were used to determine which of the two simulations provided a better fit for the actual data obtained.

The results confirmed the conclusions initially put forward by O'Connor and me. The simulation of the Eratosthenes strategy fitted the actual data much better than the memory model, and this was the case for all participants. The students actually confirmed subsequently that they had indeed used the method based on that of Eratosthenes, and again the results obtained from them and those from Michael were very similar.

After this series of studies one can conclude with some confidence that in spite of his severe mental impairments, Michael possesses exceptional numerical ability. He employs the same appropriate strategies as mathematically trained individuals and his domain-specific, high-level skill functions independently of his conceptual, linguistic and social disabilities. These impairments, in spite of his high visuospatial IQ, indicate a total lack of understanding about the meaning of things and events, and amount to something more than a circumscribed handicap. His thought processes do remain confined within a module of reasoning ability concerning space and numbers.

In this context, one needs to stress again that a high level of general intelligence seems not to be a necessary requirement for the use of an algorithm, nor is an explicit formulation essential. This was demonstrated by a calendar calculator who participated in the studies by Lisa Heavey outlined in Chapter 7. Howard had the largest span of calendar calculation in that group, and he also had the highest IQ. But even so, his verbal as well as non-verbal scores gave him an intelligence quotient in the 90s, i.e. in the low population average. However, he has a considerable arithmetical ability, including that of identifying prime numbers. When Lisa Heavey asked him about his method for doing this, he was initially quite unable to give any account of the procedures he used. But after repeated questioning over a long period of time, like the young Colburn he could eventually tell her something about his strategy. After identifying 8889 in three seconds as a non-prime, Howard, with much prompting, finally stated '3 will go into it'. For 9859, a prime number, he told Lisa after 11 seconds '3 and 7 will not go into it, 11 won't go into 9870' ($9870 - 11 = 9859$), '13 won't go into 982 and 13 will go into 39' ($982 \times 10 = 9820, 9820 + 39 = 9859$). This savant had thus tried to divide components of the given number 9859 by 3, 7, 11 and 13 in order to decide that it was a prime. When Howard was asked to find a prime number between 10500 and 10600, he came up with 10511 in less than 6 seconds. He told the investigator that 10511 was not divisible by 3 or 7. On further questioning about how he knew it could not be divided by 11 or 13, he replied '13 will go into 611 and 10511 minus 611 is 9900, and that can't be divided by 13'. Howard, like Michael, has a diagnosis of autism and, as mentioned, this condition appears to allow those who suffer from it a privileged access to segments and components of information. It was concluded from Howard's account that because of his autism he can use his cognitive style to allow him the fragmentation of target numbers into their components, which then enables him to apply possible divisors rapidly.

On some occasions Howard simply said about certain numbers that they felt like primes. But his sense of intuition was not infallible and sometimes he was mistaken. In the report by Oliver Sacks about the formidable savant twin calculators mentioned before, he observed that their calendar calculation span covered 40,000 years. However, the correctness of their date calculation could not always be checked, and neither could their prime-number generation up to those containing 12 or more digits. Interestingly, Sacks quotes a comment by Israel Rosenfield suggesting that arithmetic might not always function as a unified, modular area of ability. Instead, Rosenfield thought that the numerical domain did not need to be mentally represented as a unitary system, but could be fractionalised into 'sub-modules', perhaps developed through special interests. A similar hypothesis has been put forward here when describing individuals with sharply delineated gifts in sub-sections of the language system. It does indeed make some sense to suppose that such 'sub-modules' might especially appeal to those with autism with their predisposition towards obsessional interests in very restricted areas.

A.C. Aitkin, who is regarded as one of the most formidable mental calculators of the present century, thought of his mental calculation as 'a compound faculty' about which he was unable to provide an adequate description. However, the inability to provide an adequate account of the processes involved in extraordinary achievement does not necessarily entail a non-existence of the relevant cognitive mental representations in an abstract form. These representations can remain implicit and need not refer to their diverse observable sensory and perceptual properties, irrespective of whether they concern mathematics, music, the visual arts or language. Inspirational and cognitive processes are not mutually exclusive. The young Mozart certainly produced music of outstanding quality. Yet when as a child not yet aged three he once heard a piglet squeak, and immediately called out 'G sharp!' he thereby identified a structural feature of the musical system notwithstanding his undefinable wonderous musicianship. Thus extraordinary and seemingly mysterious special abilities do not exclude explicit or implicit awareness of the laws and structures which govern the numerical or indeed every other domain or their 'sub-domains'.

9

Drawing

My accounts of the investigations with savant artists owe much to the great art historian Sir Ernst Gombrich, and to the talks I was privileged to have had with him. He points out that of course not all pictorial representations can necessarily be designated as art. However, he also remarks that there is no generally valid definition of art, that there are only individual artists. In this brief chapter and the two that follow I will talk about those savants who have an above-average ability to produce pictures. All these individuals are autistic, and they tend to depict the concrete outside world rather than creating abstract pictorial compositions or 'conceptual' art. Yet their pictures do not merely mirror a photographic reality, though some of them often use photographs as models. Other savant artists draw from memory or from directly observed scenes, and each of them has a clearly marked personal style. I will say more about such individual characteristics in another chapter. Here I will only give some examples of drawings by the savants in our group.

All pictorial representations of the real world are transformations. Gombrich says that a picture can no more be true or false than a statement can be blue or green. Representing aspects of the real world in a picture means to adopt various kinds of schemata that create illusions. Even the process of seeing is in itself the result of a construct. All the eye transmits is a set of separate, ever-changing electrochemical impulses, which the brain organises and transforms into coherent visual percepts. Moreover, as Bartlett, one of the first great experimental psychologists pointed out as early as 1910, one not only tends to draw or paint what one *sees*, but is also influenced by what one *knows*. Thus, as Gombrich wrote, 'the innocent eye is a myth'.

Figure 9.1

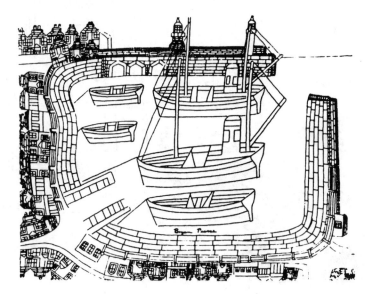

Figure 9.2

Figure 9.3

Figure 9.4

Figure 9.5

Figure 9.6

Figure 9.7

It is frequently assumed that those with autism get nearer to such an innocent eye than the rest of us, because they are much less susceptible to classifying and conceptualising the world. This is supposed to allow them to produce a purer pictorial representation of what they actually see. I will discuss this assumption in more detail in another chapter. Here, I will present a number of experiments on drawing, some of which were carried out in the 1980s with Neil O'Connor and myself, and others more recently in collaboration with Linda Pring and our research associates.

O'Connor and I started by asking what would happen if, instead of objects, savants were to match and remember or to draw abstract shapes which did not represent anything. Would the perception and memory of such non-representational models be more detailed and accurate for autistic individuals than those of other people?

We compared three groups of participants. In the first of these were eight savant artists who all had a diagnosis of autism. There were also two control groups. The savant participants were between 17 and 28 years old. Their intelligence test scores ranged from 38 to 78, and they were selected by art experts from the Institute of Education, London on the basis of their drawings. Group Two consisted of eight intellectually normal pupils from schools and colleges, whom their teachers had judged to be eligible for admission to art school. They were all over 16 years old. Individuals in Group Three had no particular drawing ability and were matched for diagnoses, age and intelligence with the savants.

We began by successively presenting each participant with series of drawings of irregular shapes, which they were told to inspect carefully. Then, without taking this model drawing away, we showed them a group of five very similar shapes, only one of which was identical in every detail to the original one. We asked them to show us which of these five shapes was the same as that in the model. We repeated this procedure with nine different shapes. So this part of the experiment was concerned with the ability to match shapes on the basis of fine discrimination of detail.

We were also interested in testing visual shape memory; thus we included a second condition in the study, using different materials. Here target shapes had to be recognised from memory rather than matched by direct comparison. Each model shape was shown for five seconds and then withdrawn. After a ten-second interval, we presented five very similar shape drawings, only one of which was identical to that seen before. The task here was the same as in the first condition, but this time the participants had to rely on their memory. We found that the group of young people with drawing ability and high IQs did better than the savants and their IQ-matched controls in both conditions. In addition, while all the participants with low intelligence and autism did better when they had to match the shapes than when recognising them, this was not so for the students with drawing abilities. It thus seemed that observation of and memory for details of non-representational shape drawings was not a general feature of savant artistic ability.

These results are of interest, because in their representational drawings savants often show an outstanding ability to reproduce details of scenes or objects that they had observed or remembered. To explore the apparent contradiction between such observations and our experimental results, we included another experiment in this series of studies. Shapes which were of course different from those shown previously had to be either directly copied or drawn from memory. Here, where drawing was involved, the results showed that all participants drew more accurately when they copied a shape directly than when they had to reproduce it from memory. However, in contrast to the previous tests where drawing had not been required, here the savants did as well on both these drawing tasks as those with similar drawing abilities but with much higher intelligence levels. The participants in Group Three who had the same intelligence levels as the savants, but had no drawing ability, performed significantly less well. Thus the key result from these drawing tests was that, in contrast to the previous conditions of shape matching and shape memory, the artistically gifted savants' performance on the drawing tasks was not determined by their intelligence but by their specific ability to draw. This indicates that savant capability was confined to the execution of that activity for which they were gifted. While intelligence apparently played a part in the observation and recognition of detail, the degree of accuracy in drawings proved to be independent of intelligence.

A point to be considered is that in these studies the materials we used had been drawings of abstract shapes, and one has to ask whether the same result would also be obtained with meaningful pictures. We therefore set out to repeat and extend our results in another study. The same eight savants participated in this, and the comparison groups were the same eight intellectually normal artistically gifted young people and the eight autistic controls without a special drawing ability. Line drawings of objects were each shown for five seconds and then removed. The task was to decide whether a second picture shown ten seconds after the first was either the same as the first or different from it only in one small detail. In another condition, the pictured object had to be drawn from memory. The results confirmed the previous finding. The detailed visual recognition memory of pictured objects by the savants and by their IQ-matched controls was worse than that of the normal intelligent participants with drawing ability. But again, savants did not differ from the more intelligent participants in their ability to draw the objects accurately from memory. Not surprisingly, both these groups with drawing ability were superior in this respect to the controls matched for intelligence levels with the savants.

O'Connor and I included another previously unexplored variable in this series of experiments. Drawing, though guided by vision, is essentially a motor activity carried out by arm and hand movements. We wondered whether it was only visual features that were accurately reproduced in drawings by those who had a graphic ability, or whether the appropriate movement patterns would also be well retained. In order to test this we produced shapes that were made from raised wires on a flat surface. The participants were blindfolded and asked to trace around these with their fingers. After they had done this, we removed the blindfolds and asked them to recognise or draw what they had just traced.

Interestingly, the pattern of results reflected those obtained in the previous studies. Only when the traced picture had subsequently to be drawn did both normal and savants artists perform very similarly, and significantly better than the non-artistic intellectually retarded group. Thus, irrespective of whether the participants had seen or traced around the model shapes, the savants could draw them from memory as well as their intellectually normal-functioning artistically gifted counterparts.

Our conclusion from that series of studies with a group of savant artists was that only when they were actually drawing did they do better than others with the same diagnoses and intelligence levels.

This is reminiscent of the findings from the investigation of date memory with savant calendar calculators. There, Lisa Heavey found that these savants showed a better memory for day–date pairings they had previously calculated than for those they had simply studied. There again, better memory was related to the actual activity for which the savants had a specific ability.

In his book *Art and Illusion: A Study in the Psychology of Pictorial Presentations*, Gombrich states that drawing is an activity, and therefore the artist tends to look more at what he does than at what he sees. The findings from this series of studies suggest that this statement holds as true for savants as it does for artists in general.

Plate 1 'Empire State Building'

Plate 2 'View of Los Angeles'

Plate 3a 'Tropicl Fish' (drawing)

Plate 3b 'Tropicl Fish'

Plate 4a 'Mountains and Flowers' (drawing)

Plate 4b 'Mountains and Flowers' (photograph)

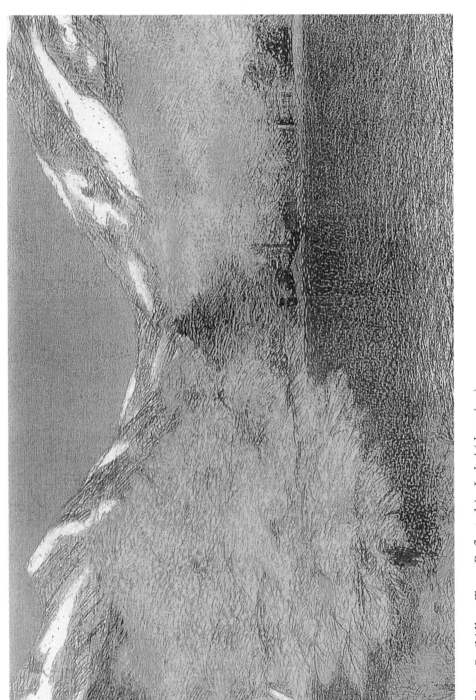

Plate 5a 'Yellow Trees Reflected in Lake' (drawing)

Plate 5b 'Yellow Trees Reflected in Lake' (photograph)

Plate 6a 'Standing Rock Against Mountain' (drawing)

Plate 6b 'Standing Rock Against Mountain' (photograph)

10

Pictorial Strategies

I will begin this further brief account on savant artists by reporting the results of a study that appeared to link an enhanced ability to segment a pattern into its constituent parts to a talent for drawing. Linda Pring and I compared four groups of participants on their performance on the block design test, mentioned previously. It forms part of one of the most renowned tests of general intelligence. The task is to reconstruct a complex compound pattern from separate blocks, each showing a segment of the total design (see p.47). We tested four groups, the first containing those savant artists who had taken part in the previous set of studies. The second group contained students from a university art department, while the members of the other two groups had no specific artistic skill and were respectively matched for intelligence with members of the two talented groups.

I have mentioned that those with autism tend to do better on the block design test than one would expect from their general intelligence levels. The questions we asked here were whether an ability to reconstruct a pattern from its separate elements would be even more marked in autistic savant artists, and whether this would also be the case for the art students. It was found that both the savants and the art students did better on this test than the participants without a specific artistic skill. It thus seems that an enhanced ability to segment a pattern into its parts, as well as to reconstruct it subsequently, is not only related to an artistic talent of those with autism, but also evident in normally functioning, artistically gifted individuals.

Following this preliminary investigation into the efficient strategy for reconstructing a pattern from its parts, Linda Pring and I turned to investigating whether the savants would be able to use two pictorial devices that had been crucial in traditional Western art. One of these was *linear perspective* and the other was the *ignoring of perceptual size constancy.*

Illusions of three-dimensional space on a two-dimensional surface had already been obtained in wall paintings at Pompeii and elsewhere by the skilful variation of light and shade as well as by foreshortening. But it was only during the Italian Renaissance that the laws of linear perspective based on precise geometry were formulated. One of these basic principles is that whenever lines in the real, three-dimensional world run away from the viewer in parallel (e.g. railway lines), they must converge in a picture in order to give an illusion of depth. Eventually these converging lines should, if continued long enough, meet at a single 'vanishing point' on the horizon. The location of this point depends on the distance of the eye from the plane.

Another pictorial device is to ignore perceptual size constancy with increasing distance. The optical size of an object in space decreases proportionally with its distance from the viewer. But this changing size of the image on the retina of the eye is not the only guide to our perception. We also take account of our experience of object size and knowledge of distance, which allows our brains to create a relatively stable visual world. Thus, a friend walking away from us does not appear half his real size when his distance from us has doubled. Size constancy allows us to compromise between the optical image and our knowledge, and the resulting percept does not give us the impression of a continuously shrinking and growing world. It is only when distance becomes very large, like for instance looking at the stars or a plane in the sky, that we see these as very much smaller than we know they really are. However, in Western pictorial art, perceptual size constancy has been largely ignored. Thus the artist will indicate increasing distance from the viewer by proportionally decreasing the object's size on his pictures. On a two-dimensional surface the illusion of spatial depth is created by dispensing with the normally operating perceptual mechanism of size constancy, reflecting instead more closely the optical size of the depicted objects. Both linear perspective (i.e. the gradual convergence in a picture of parallels in the real world for creating a illusion of depth) and the abandoning of perceptual size constancy (when indicating three-dimensional space and distance) have been part of our traditional pictorial vocabulary until they were abandoned by Picasso.

Linda Pring and I assessed whether savant artists would spontaneously use these two pictorial devices (linear perspective and reduced size constancy) in drawings for which no models were provided. Nine savant artists, all of them autistic, and nine children of normal intelligence who were gifted in drawing took part in this study. As previously, all participants were judged by art experts and teachers to show evidence of artistic talent. The savants were aged between 17 and 29 years and their mental ages, as obtained on a spatial reasoning test, ranged from 8 to 13 years. The chronological age of the non-autistic artists covered the same age range as the savants' mental age; thus, they were children aged between 8 and 13 years. Each participant was given a piece of A4 portrait-style paper and asked to draw a road that started at the bottom of the paper next to them and ended far away at the top of the sheet. After they had done this, we told them to draw three cars on this picture of the road. One of these should be nearest to them (i.e. at the bottom of the sheet), one in the middle distance, and one far away near the road's end.

An art expert evaluated these drawings without knowing which were produced by savants and which by the schoolchildren. The results of this evaluation were that eight of the nine savants and all nine of the control children drew the road borders as converging lines that would eventually have met at a vanishing point. It is of interest that the one savant who drew two parallel lines to indicate the borders of the road had one of the highest IQs of the group, thus confirming the independence of intelligence from savant drawing ability. Regarding the breakup of size constancy, seven savant artists and eight of the nine controls drew the cars in decreasing size with increasing distance. The statistical analysis showed no significant group differences in using linear perspective and in ignoring perceptual size constancy.

The results of this study clearly indicated that these tested pictorial rules were employed with equal efficiency by savant artists and by those of higher intelligence who had a gift for drawing. It appears that all artistically talented participants had extracted such devices to portray three-dimensional space on a two-dimensional surface from an environment abounding with pictorial representations, such as posters, illustrations, etc. It should be remembered that no models were presented here, and those features which were tested belonged to a specific pictorial vocabulary underlying the performance of both savant artists and artistically gifted normal children.

I will now turn to somewhat different issues concerning pictorial strategies. In the following set of studies O'Connor and I had been interested in how savant drawings would be affected by different conditions under which they had be executed. We thus compared a group of autistic savant artists with artistically gifted children of the same mental ages. The first set of drawings had to be produced from a three-dimensional model scene put on a table in front of the participants. In the second condition this was replaced by a photograph of the model. Here, a conversion from a three- to a two-dimensional scene had already occurred, which might allow the artists to concentrate more on the artistic quality of the drawing than on representing a three-dimensional model on a two-dimensional surface. For the third set of drawings the model was removed altogether and had to be drawn from memory. This would allow even more freedom for transforming what had actually been seen into a picture that was determined by an individual's artistic style and preference. Finally, we put the three-dimensional model back on the table in front of the artists, and asked them to draw not what they themselves saw, but instead to represent the view of someone sitting at a 90-degree angle from the participant; thus not having a front view but a side view of the model.

This last condition was of particular interest because, as outlined, those with autism largely lack the ability to appreciate that other people's thoughts, beliefs and opinions might differ from those held by themselves. From a series of innovative investigations Frith and her colleagues had concluded that autistic individuals lacked a 'theory of mind'. Interestingly, Steven Mitner, a professor of early prehistory, has recently put forward his conclusion, based on archaeological artefacts, that humans had only begun to understand the thought processes of other people about 30,000 years ago. But, sadly, autistic individuals seem to have missed out on this evolutionary development. In our study we had asked whether autistic savant artists were not only 'mind blind' but also 'view blind'.

Figure 10.1 shows the model and Figure 10.2 is one of the savant drawings produced from it. The drawing by a savant illustrated in Figure 10.3 was done from a photograph; another savant drew Figure 10.4 from memory; and Figure 10.5, as if from another person's angle of viewing, is yet another savant drawing. These drawings by different savant artists clearly indicate individual styles and preferences, as well as increased freedom according to the condition under which they were executed. All drawings were assessed for their artistic quality by members of the London University Institute of Education's art department. Five different pictorial aspects were taken into consideration and rated separately on a scale from 1 to 5. One such rating referred to the liveliness and sensitivity of the drawn objects, and the second to vitality of line and texture. The other criteria were the degree at which a distinct

Figure 10.1 Model

Figure 10.2 Drawing from model

Figure 10.3 Drawing from photo

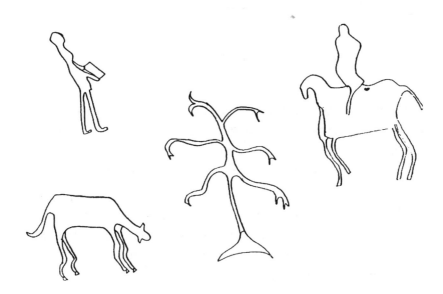

Figure 10.4 Drawing from memory

Figure 10.5 Drawing from other viewpoint

personal style was evident, the organisation and composition of the drawing and the extent to which a compelling image was produced. The results of this rating procedure revealed no differences in any of these qualities between the two participating artistically gifted groups.

The finding of special interest is the one obtained when the artists were asked to draw an image of how a scene would look from some other angle of viewing than that of the artist. This was done by the autistic as successfully as by the artistically gifted normal participants. Thus the savants gave no indication of being 'view blind'. Some tentative but interesting conclusions can be drawn from this result. Nearly all savants are autistic, and therefore impaired in the appreciation of other people's thoughts, beliefs and feelings. However, when such autistic individuals are artistically gifted, they can draw a scene not only as they themselves see it, but also as how it might appear from somebody else's perspective. Thus, as with other savant gifts, mental processes that might not be evident in other behavioural areas become manifest in those activities which are directly talent related. Of course, one must not ignore the fact that a mental representation of other people's states of mind differs from those of their positional point of view in subtle but crucial aspects. To adopt and draw the latter does not necessitate relating to another person's mental state. When we first met Stephen, the savant artist I have already mentioned, he drew for us a picture of a road accident he had witnessed as if seen from a rooftop and not as he had actually observed it on the road. Other aspects of a specific artistic vocabulary are also available to autistic savants gifted in drawing, as shown by their spontaneous use of linear perspective and the ignoring of perceptual size constancy when producing a picture. Thus it appeared that the drawings by the autistic savants were by no means restricted to what they saw, or had seen, but demonstrated as much artistic freedom as those by the control participants.

In his book *Inner Vision: An Exploration of Art and the Brain*, Semir Zeka made it clear that the areas and mechanisms of brain activity do differ according to whether a picture is produced or is understood. He cites the case of a patient who after a stroke had difficulties with seeing objects, but could do a drawing of St Paul's Cathedral in three-dimensional perspective. However, though he could see and describe the details of this picture, such as the slant of the lines, he could not combine such separate elements in his own drawing into a whole, and thus failed to recognise what he had drawn. His implicit knowledge of objects and of drawings representing them had been destroyed. D.D. Hoffman linked the rules of visual perception to those of Noam Chomsky's 'universal grammar' as he describes in his book *Visual Intelligence: How We Create What We See*. Thus we integrate lines, depths, colour, form and motion into 'seeing'. Perception is a process of connecting and transforming separate visual stimuli. But in representational art these elements have again to be segmented into their components for the creation of a total image. As early as the 1930s, the American psychologist J.J. Gibson had already pointed out that seeing the world as a picture was an alternative to that of normal perception. I like to propose that the findings I have presented here allow us to conclude that even autistic savant artists have this alternative available to them.

11

Two Savant Artists

Gombrich relates that in his autobiography the artist Ludwig Richter had recalled how in the 1820s he and three of his young friends had gone out together, each to draw the same scene 'without diverting a hair's breadth from what they saw'. But though they had faithfully kept to this pact, the result was four totally different pictures. Richter concluded from this experience that objective pictorial rendering was an impossibility. Forms, colours, light and their interrelationships would always be portrayed according to an individual's unique personality and temperament.

Artistic styles do also vary, of course, because of different national and cultural environments and the development of new stylistic movements over time. These factors interact with individual preferences and predispositions. One such stylistic distinction has been outlined by Heinrich Wölfflin. In his book *Principles of Art History*, which was first published in 1915, Wölfflin, who is by many regarded as the founder of modern art history, analysed two basic styles in Western visual art, which he called 'the linear' and 'the painterly'. It is because aspects of these stylistic characteristics are evident in the work of the two savant artists described here that I like to mention Wölfflin's definitions in some little detail. Thus according to him the linear style became prominent in the Italian Renaissance during the fifteenth century. When Brunelleschi and Alberti formulated the laws of linear perspective by which pictorial space could be rendered as optically continuous and mathematically coherent, Masaccio painted a fresco in which the illusion of the continuity between real and pictorial space was complete. In the paintings and frescos of this period, separate objects retain their distinctiveness and independence through being bordered by clear continuous contours. Colour is mainly used to emphasise the shapes that these outlines create. Thus in the linear style, line and contour dominate.

In Venice the Renaissance began somewhat later than in Florence and Rome. Here, what Wölfflin called the painterly style was developed and became subsequently dominant in the 1600s during the Baroque period. Initially, its dominance of light, tone and colour was probably influenced by Venice's endless shifting play of light that creates appearances of form without substance. In the painterly style, lines become indistinct and sometimes disappear altogether. In their place, colour and light dominate, overriding distinctive individual shapes. This lack of linear definition creates an atmospheric elusiveness and, according to Wölfflin, this indefiniteness is the essence of the 'painterly'. Wölfflin's stylistic distinctions not only apply to different periods of time such as the Renaissance or the Baroque, but can also be seen as characterising different artists from the same historical period. Thus among the painters of the nineteenth century Ingres is often described as the master of immaculate line and Delacroix as excelling in his superb brush strokes. Wölfflin used his terms of linear and painterly styles not only in regard to pictures but also as applying equally to sculpture and architecture.

The reader may feel that it is inappropriate to link the modest achievements of savant artists with such illustrious movements and names. I do think, however, that the distinction between linear and painterly styles has some applicability to the work of the two savants to be described here. As I have pointed out, cultural, environmental and personal factors generally interact to produce stylistic differences. However, here we are dealing with autistic individuals who usually have no spontaneous interest in, and are often unaware of, what goes on in the arts around them. They frequently even dislike looking at other artists' work and their differing styles must therefore be regarded as primarily an expression of their individual skills, preferences and temperaments. Michael Buhler, a painter who teaches at the City and Guilds of London Art School, assessed the examples of work by the two savants to be discussed in this chapter. We were unable to arrange a repetition of Richter's experiment, and therefore these two artists did not attempt pictorial representations at the same time or of the same scenes. Nevertheless, they demonstrate that Wölfflin's stylistic distinctions can be validly applied to the work of autistic savant artists.

When Neil O'Connor and I first met Stephen, he was 15 years old and attended a school for children with severe learning difficulties. His headteacher Loraine Cole and art teacher Chris Morris had come to hear of our savant research and told us of his extraordinary drawing ability. But from early in his life his development had been delayed. He sat, stood and walked late and seemed to develop no language at all. He did not like to be picked up and cuddled, and never seemed to look at people. Later on he did not play with other children, including his sister two years older than him, and he was diagnosed as suffering from autism and impaired mental development. But when aged six, he became absorbed with drawing and produced remarkable pictures of buildings, cars and townscapes from memory, which he had only briefly seen. It was clear from the very start that his talent for drawing was extraordinary.

When we first tested his intelligence when aged 15, he had a verbal reasoning ability of a normal seven to eight year old. However, his visuospatial intelligence was near the normal average. Subsequently, the BBC approached us to produce a film on our work with savants in which Stephen participated. This film, *The Foolish Wise Ones*, created a wide interest in the savant phenomenon and in particular in Stephen's drawings. It brought him to the attention of Margaret Hewson, who began to take a great interest in his artistic and personal development. She obtained commissions for him, organised exhibitions of his work, published books of his drawings and took him on journeys all over the world. Stephen took to her from the start, and he owes her a very great deal, including his eventual admission to the City and Guilds of London Art School.

Figure 11.1 'Trip on the river'

From the time we first met Stephen, we had been especially impressed by his vivid and dynamic style of line drawing and his superb intuitive ability to portray spatial relationships and depth. Two of his early drawings, 'Trip on the River' (Figure 11.1) and 'St Paul's Cathedral' (Figure 11.2), illustrate this. In 'Trip on the River' Stephen uses lines that are variously spaced for tonal values. Lines also indicate the moving river and the trees along the embankment. There is relatively little emphasis on a carefully balanced total composition, instead the drawing gives the impression of movement and spontaneity. 'St Paul's Cathedral' is an energetic drawing

Figure 11.2 'St Pauls Cathedral'

executed in linear style. Variation of tone is again obtained through variously spaced lines that maintain their separate distinctiveness. Though portraying a static building, the picture conveys the dynamism that Stephen brings to this linear idiom.

Linearity had remained characteristic of Stephen's work until his entry into art school. Up to that time he had hardly used shading or colour. But his teachers took the view that though of course it was necessary to have regard for his personal, emotional and intellectual characteristics, a wide 'artistic vocabulary' (i.e. different pictorial techniques and idioms) should always be taught. These could then be used according to each artist's own intentions. Thus, in order to enlarge Stephen's artistic range, he was first entered into a painting class.

As has been stated, a linear style focuses on contours, the relationship of edges and the spaces between them, whilst to obtain a painterly effect, tone and colour will dominate. A marked tonal difference may serve to reduce the pictorial space, while a small tonal contrast between objects will make them seem to recede into the distance. If tones are closely related this can give the impression of harmony, while tonal contrast may make a dramatic impact. Thus, through the selection of tonal values the artist may extend or reduce his pictorial space; and what aspects of this method he selects to apply will determine the impression the picture creates.

At first Stephen seemed puzzled when asked to point to the brightest and darkest tones on a glass bottle, but after a scale of tones from white to black was shown to him, and it was explained that the different shades were called 'tones', he quickly grasped the concept. Thereafter he acquired the use of tonal values with a striking speed, which was well above that of some of his fellow students. His use of this technique is illustrated here in the drawing of boxes and in a figure drawing from life.

In 'Still Life of Boxes' (Figure 11.3) Stephen has used lines to demarcate the edges, but the drawing could have been done with no outlines at all. The perspective is adequate but not strictly

Figure 11.3 'Still life of boxes'

accurate, especially on the shadow side of the foreground box. The use of tone does the job without subtlety or close observation. The same comments apply to 'Nude' (Figure 11.4), though here Stephen shows no problems in observing and recording. But individual stylistic characteristics are missing and though confronted with a nude, he still seemed not to get interested in this project. These tonal pictures are typical competent art student's work, but seem to lack the dynamic impact of Stephen's earlier spontaneous line drawings. Of course, such a temporary loss of personal style is not unusual during early art school training. It is often only later that a student develops the ability to use his acquired pictorial vocabulary for his own purposes and intentions.

Regarding colour, though able to match those of the models in his pictures, Stephen's teacher felt that he did not love colour for its own sake. If, for instance, he included a bright yellow colour in his

Figure 11.4 'Nude'

painting of a New York street scene, he said that he did this because he liked the yellow taxicabs of the city, rather than in order to give a bright accent to his picture. His colouring appeared to be determined by what he saw, rather than by a desire to give emphasis and modulation to what he painted. Every colour that was in a scene went into his picture regardless of its effect, and there was no indication of an aesthetically determined selectivity.

In Stephen's second year on this course, one project required the students first to produce a random pattern of coloured non-representational shapes. Then they were each given a different cue word according to which they had to transform their abstract picture into an illustration of this word. Stephen's teacher was initially doubtful whether he would understand this task requirement, but it so happened that Stephen was given the word 'earthquake' as his title, a phenomenon which had always fascinated him. He did transform his abstract into a vivid and evocative picture of an earthquake, showing burning buildings, crushed cars and running people. This clearly illustrated that when his interest and imagination were caught, he could do more than reproduce what he had seen. He demonstrated that he could generate images and project them on to random coloured shapes, thus transforming them into meaningful, coherent pictorial representations. Though it was still felt that he was unlikely to initiate such an undertaking himself, had few aesthetic intentions and had merely followed instructions, the results of this project nevertheless demonstrate that his artistic potential goes beyond the mere reproduction of what he had perceived or remembered having seen.

For his last year at art school Stephen was transferred from the painting course to one of graphics and printmaking, teaching mainly etching and linocut. Perhaps it was no surprise to those who were familiar with his early spontaneously produced line drawings that he seemed much more at home in this idiom than in that of painting. In the linocut 'Empire State Building' (Plate 1), the print shows a competent and intelligent view of the medium, especially in the dark green foreground reaching up into the denser areas of yellow light. Horizontal lines in the sky are used to dilute the intensity of the yellow colour with white. The etching 'View of Los Angeles' (Plate 2) was done freely from a photograph. Stephen's centralised composition conveys a sense of space through the grid of the receding diagonals of the streets and houses. Though the print could have been done in various colour combinations,

Stephen did not seem to have strong preferences in this respect. But he produced a subtle evocation of the city through the strictly linearly arranged foreground, while the vertically rising skyscrapers in the background merge into the evening light of the sky.

Stephen clearly remains a predominantly graphic artist, most at home with the linear style by which he is able to express his own temperament, his preferences and his particular skill. His artistic talent thus remains most evident in the idiom that he had originally and spontaneously selected. This conclusion is reminiscent of one stated by Leon Miller in regard to the young savant musician Eddie, whom he described in detail in his outstanding book, *Musical Savants*. Miller's studies of Eddie took place before, as well as during, the time when he had begun to take music lessons. But Miller found no evidence that his performance showed any consequences of such training, and he concluded that it was unlikely that formal teaching had changed Eddie's spontaneous musicianship in any fundamental way. Similarly, it seems likely that Stephen will retain his initial artistic identity. His outstanding ability when using his own preferred medium is convincingly illustrated in an earlier drawing 'The Reading Room in the British Museum' (Figure 11.7), which allowed him to put specific emphasis on three-dimensional space and detailed linear composition. It is an excellent drawing, showing a superb grasp of perspective, especially evident in the windows of the dome and the central circular shelves, which though slightly distorted do not spoil the total sense of space. On the contrary, a certain degree of distortion can be expressive, and in this picture the leaning of the shelves towards the viewer emphasises the circularity of the whole structure. The drawing is wholly linear and achieves tonality by the density of the lines depicting the books and the shelves. The scene is enlivened by people walking about, and especially by the pretty girl in the foreground.

However, though Stephen's talent remains most evident in his line drawings, there is no doubt that he has profited from his art

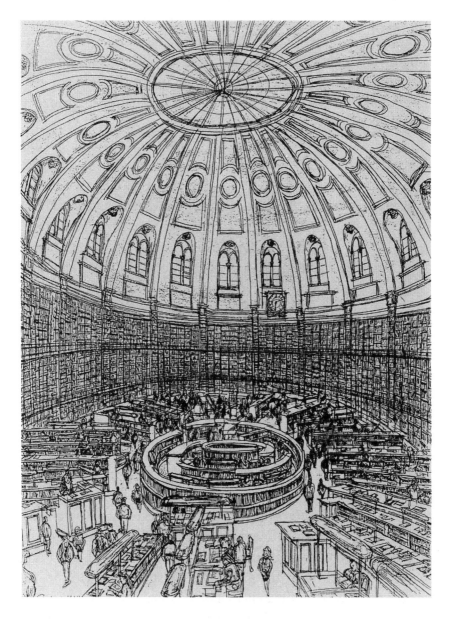

Figure 11.7 'The Reading Room in the British Museum'

school teaching. His scope for exploration has been enhanced by an increased artistic repertoire of techniques, and this gives him the chance to select his own pictorial vocabulary with more conscious effectiveness in the future. It will now be up to him how he will employ his enlarged artistic range to develop his outstanding potential talent. One would expect though that his chosen preference would always be for a linear style, which must be regarded as his native pictorial language.

Richard, the second savant artist whose work I will be discussing, was born in 1952. When he was one month old, bilateral congenital cataract was diagnosed and some heart dysfunction was noticed. At age six he developed lymphosarcoma, though this responded well to treatment. At 18 it was found that he suffered from insulin-dependent diabetes, which appears to have caused some additional retinal damage. He also developed hypothyroidism and glaucoma, but these are well controlled with medication. As Richard is also extremely myopic and his distance vision in one eye is reduced to 4/60 and in the other to 3/60, he is quite clearly a severely physically handicapped individual.

He began to talk and walk late and had very clumsy movements. When he finally began to speak, his language was restricted to noun-verb utterances, leaving out linking words. He was subsequently admitted to an occupation centre for children with severe learning difficulties, which he attended from the age of 6 to 15. When he was first tested for his mental development at age 11, he was found to have a reasoning ability about equal to that of a three and a half year old normal child. But more recently we obtained a verbal IQ of 47 and a non-verbal one of 55. Thus at the beginning of this investigation of his artistic talent undertaken by Linda Pring and me, together with our research associate Pamela Heaton, his mental age was approximately that of a normal eight-year-old. The psychiatrist Sula Wolff from Edinburgh University had noted earlier that he had never played with toys or with other children, but tended to walk aimlessly about the classroom. At the start of our study she confirmed her initial diagnosis of autism by formal assessment. Richard lives at home with devoted, loving parents, and his father does everything to support his artistic talent, which became evident when he was four years old. Since then, Richard has continuously produced pictures. His outstanding artistic ability clearly demonstrates the modular nature of a talent that is independent of his other considerable disabilities.

He uses oil-based crayons on paper and his pictures are mostly based on landscape photographs which he has seen earlier in travel offices and libraries. Sometimes he also draws natural scenes, either directly or from memory, which he has looked at through binoculars. He travels widely with his father, often to open exhibitions of his work, and he sells his pictures to a wide audience; for instance, Baroness Margaret Thatcher has been an admiring member. He will often talk about the countries he has visited, their flags, currencies, temperatures and local times. In our study we attempted to compare Richard's pictures with the photographic models from which they were derived, and were helped in their assessment by Michael Buhler.

Richard works with his eyes very close to the paper. His method is to begin with an overall coloured surface such as a blue sky or a green meadow. He proceeds to draw mountains, trees, etc. on top of this, then adds flowers or houses, which he will again cover with more detail. He thus applies layer after layer of colour, going from an overall covering background to more and more detailed representations. He can apply this method successfully, as his exclusive use of oil pastels gives sufficient covering power to make it possible. It must be left an open question whether Richard starts with an approximate plan of the whole picture or whether he decides to add detail as he goes along. However, as the pictures shown here were all done from memory of previously seen photographs, it appears probable that his starting point was a total reconstructed memory representation. To the question why a mentally handicapped autistic individual with severely impaired vision should enthusiastically pursue the creation of pictures, there is of course no conclusive answer. But it seems likely that Richard's visual limitations interact with his memory to transform a more detailed, sharper edged reality into unified pictorial images which are dominated by colour and light.

In 'Tropical Fish' (Plate 3a) the plants and fish are very much enlarged in comparison with those in the photograph (Plate 3b). They dominate the composition, which is now slanted horizontally rather than diagonally. The underwater perspective has become much clearer and the white light around the plants creates an effect of luminosity that is absent in the model.

'Mountains and Flowers' (Plate 4a) gives a brighter and sunnier impression of the scene than the photograph (Plate 4b). The mountain is no longer looming rather threateningly over the dark foreground, but is merging with the sky. Its contours are less rugged but have been unified and softened. The flowers have become much more dominant by extending the foreground and now dominate the picture.

'Yellow Trees Reflected in Lake' (Plate 5a) gives a much more elusive shape to the trees' reflection in the lake than the photograph (Plate 5b). The overall composition is simplified and the tree line now echoes the shape of the mountain range. The snow on the mountaintop adds brightness and the craggy details of the mountainside have been softened by omitting detail. The picture generates a lyrical, poetic mood that is not present in the photograph.

In 'Standing Rock Against Mountain' (Plate 6a), the simplification of the rock's surface detail and overall shape gives it a more abstract, less realistic appearance than the photograph (Plate 6b). Its dark tone connects with a deepened shadow on the mountainside, while the bright yellow flowers in the foreground add colour. The shape of the mountain's snow-top is also simplified and the overall impression of the picture is both more dramatic and yet less threatening than in the model.

As can be seen from these examples of Richard's work, his painterly style allows colour to function without interruption over large areas, unifying the overall compositions, thus giving an impression of harmony and light. He produces subtle effects of atmospheric perspective, colour blending and luminosity. His softening of shapes and the omission of details contribute to balanced and unified pictorial representations, thereby transforming the models from which they are derived.

Though I know of no other visual artist who suffers from combined physical and mental impairments to the same degree as Richard, there are reports of great painters with quite severe visual handicaps. Trevor-Roper has given a vivid account of some of these in his book about *The World Through Blinded Sight*. Thus Cézanne, like Richard, was a diabetic, and this added further retinal damage to his initial myopia. Trevor-Roper quotes this comment made by a contemporary on Cézanne's pictures: 'An incomplete talent with an incomplete vision resulted in works that were always incomplete and sketchy.' But Cézanne himself, when persuaded to look through correcting spectacles, had exclaimed: 'Take these vulgar things away!' He clearly preferred his own view of the world. Trevor-Roper also reports a charming anecdote of Monet, who was very myopic in his late years. When he was made to look through glasses, he is reported to have said: 'My God, I see like Bouguereau.' Bouguereau was a conventionally naturalistic painter of the period. It seems that these great innovative artists used the freedom that their undefined perceptions gave them to impose their own stylistic individuality on their art.

Richard usually creates his pictures from memory, rather than from direct perception. But memory does not consist of a reactivation of existing traces, but is primarily an imaginative, active process of reconstruction. As a consequence, perceptions and experiences undergo transformation in memory representations and, as I have already pointed out, in Richard's case these interact with an initially rather undefined perception. These factors together with his specific skill and preference result in his distinctive and personal pictorial style, which in Wölfflin's terms is clearly painterly. Contours are largely dissolved and replaced by surfaces on which light and colours merge. In his writing about Venetian artists, Ruskin had said that perception of colour is a gift as definitely granted to one person, as an ear for music is to another. Richard certainly has this gift. Pictorial spaces in terms of colour and light variations are represented by him in a near abstract form. Shapes are dissolved and nature is represented in a similar way to that of the school of the 'Sublime' in landscape painting. He creates harmonious worlds that differ, for example, from that of Romantic art, which tends to depict an often threatening nature. Richard achieves subtle effects of atmospheric perspective and colour blending that create an impression of luminescence. In typically painterly style, there is little emphasis on detailed, structural features. In his pictures colour and light are allowed to function over large areas without interruption, creating a unified impression of atmospheric harmony.

Having compared the pictures of these two savant artists, both suffering from autism and cognitive handicaps, it is clear that the stylistic characteristics of their pictures could not be more different. Stephen, using a typically linear approach, has a superb sense of perspective and an extraordinary ability to observe, remember and portray detailed features of a scene. Richard omits such details, as well as distinct lines and contours and obtains his rather lyrical effect through a fusion of light and colour.

One of Wölfflin's arguments about the linear and painterly styles is of interest in our context because it seems to contradict the frequently expressed view about the work of autistic artists such as Stephen. It is often said that such talented individuals tend to portray in their pictures what they see or remember having seen; no more nor less. But Wölfflin points out that 'seeing' is relative. Differently sized objects require a different distance of the viewer from the object, in order to be seen with the same clarity. However, for instance, in Holbein's portraits the finest details of a lace collar or a gold embroidery on a dress are given with the same detailed clarity as are much larger or nearer forms. This is not what the artist would have seen if he kept his position in relation to his model constant. Thus Holbein painted things as he knew they were, not as he saw them. Similarly, the boundaries between the books in the far away shelves in the library as drawn by Stephen, could not have been an accurate reflection of what he actually saw. The same is true of the clear details in the ceiling. He would have had to change his position constantly in order to see all these features with the same clarity and definition. In contrast, in the painterly style things are treated not as they are but as they seem, not as realities but as appearances. According to such an argument, it is Richard's pictures that reflect what he sees, and it is Stephen who draws not so much what he sees, but what he knows things to be really like. Of course, nothing of this entails that one stylistic approach is superior to the other. They simply offer different solutions to the problems artists have in representing their own personal realities.

For stating my conclusions on these issues, I can do no better than to quote E.H. Gombrich's English version of a poem by Friedrich Nietzsche, the German poet and philosopher who lived in the second part of the nineteenth century. He wrote:

> *All nature faithfully — but by what feint*
> *Can nature be subdued to arts constraint?*
> *Her smallest fragment is still infinite!*
> *And so he paints but what he likes in it.*
> *What does he like? He likes what he can paint.*

12

Musical Memory and Improvisation

Music draws on a multitude of functions including among others those of invention, execution, cognition, emotion, communication and aesthetics. This multidimensional appeal has made music a universal phenomenon in all of human history, perhaps only comparable to that of language. But while language usually refers to something outside itself, music need refer to nothing but itself. It is autonomous, and it is this self-reference of music that the painter Vasily Kandinsky wanted to achieve through abstract visual art. In view of its abstract character, it is therefore of particular interest that music is one area in which savants excel.

One of the earliest published accounts of a musical savant was given in 1886 by Edward Seguin. In his classic book *Idiocy: Its Treatment by the Physiological Method* he described a blind slave boy with very limited verbal and reasoning abilities, who had nevertheless effortlessly acquired an extensive piano repertoire. 'Blind Tom' gave many concert performances and his playing was described as extraordinary. Though no formal assessment of his intelligence exists, it seems established that there was a wide discrepancy between his musical talent and his other abilities. Many savant musicians are congenitally blind, autistic or both, as well as cognitively impaired, and early accounts frequently suggest that such individuals show a strong interest in music very early in their lives. Here I would like to describe studies with savant musicians that were carried out by O'Connor and myself together with our collaborators.

The first of these studies investigated the musical memory of a savant pianist. Noel had attended nursery school from the age of nine months up to five years, after which he was placed into a school for children with severe learning difficulties. O'Connor and I met him after a colleague told us about his outstanding musical ability. While at school, he did not make contact with the other children, nor did he initiate speech, and he showed the typically autistic pattern of repetitive and obsessive behaviour. After leaving school he was admitted to a residential centre for people with autism. Noel had no musical instrument at home, but listened for hours to the radio. Whenever he had access to the school piano, he would play by ear what he had heard on the previous evening.

Musical components such as melodic structures, harmonic relationships, scale and key constraints as well as rhythm and timing may all or in part be extracted by the listener and retained in musical memory. Because of this multitude of variables it seemed of interest to analyse Noel's musical memory more closely. Together with our colleague John Sloboda, who is an accomplished musician as well as a pyschologist, we therefore decided to carry out the following study when Noel was 19 years old. He then had an IQ of 61 and still an almost total absence of spontaneous speech.

We played two pieces of recorded music to him as well as to a professional pianist, which as far as we could ascertain were previously unknown to both participants. One was Grieg's 'Melody', Opus 47 No. 3, and the second was part of Bartok's *Mikrokosmos*. Each musician heard and played the Grieg music first and was told to listen to it carefully and try to remember it, as he would be asked to play it later.

Throughout musical history people have attempted to order and divide ranges of sounds into steps which would provide a basis for music. Like almost all Western music between 1600 and 1900, Grieg's 'Melody' is composed in classical diatonic form. This contains two different types of scale, the major and the minor. The term 'scale' indicates that there are steps between successive notes such as on a ladder or staircase, and in diatonic scales these are usually a mixture of tones and semitones. While the position of differently sized intervals (i.e. whole and half tones) is fixed in the major scales, the sequence of whole- and half-tone steps can be more variable in the minor. Traditionally, music in the major mode has been taken to convey positive, bright moods and in the minor to give darker and sadder impressions. Diatonic music usually contains themes which are repeated with different elaborations and variations.

First, a recording of 'Melody' was played through from beginning to end to each musician. Then it was played in short sections and after each such hearing the participants had to play this back together with those parts they had previously heard. When at the end of this procedure each pianist had played as much of the whole piece as he could remember, Noel gave an almost note-perfect rendering of all 64 bars of 'Melody'. The harmonic as well as the melodic components had been retained by him and he played overall 798 notes of which only 8 per cent were wrong. In contrast the professional pianist attempted to play only 354 notes, but in this much abbreviated version there was a total of 80 per cent wrong notes. Moreover, after 24 hours during which Noel had not heard the piece again, he gave a second near-perfect performance.

However, as I have stated earlier, the primary interest in our savant research was not simply to ascertain *what* extraordinary things such people could do, but rather *how* such achievements were accomplished. What were the characteristics of this amazing memory? Kanner had initially observed that those with autism could frequently remember apparently unconnected items or events outstandingly well. Many autistic children 'echo back' long passages of speech they have heard, though they have little language understanding. Could it be the case that savants' remembering of music was also simply 'echoic'? We had already been able to demonstrate that savant calendar calculators drew on an extensive day–date memory ranging over many years, and remembered a great number of individual dates. But we had also found that they used the calendar's rule-governed structure to help them in their calculations. Moreover, this was the case regardless of whether or not they could state such rules. Was it possible that savant musicians recognised and remembered equivalent musical structures? We thought that one way to learn more about their musical strategy was to analyse not only how many or how few, but what kind of errors were made by our pianists.

Overall, Noel had made 54 mistakes and the control 265. Noel's errors were largely in the melody, whereas the harmony was almost note perfect. A detailed analysis showed that most of his mistakes were actually not the playing of wrong notes, but omissions of repeating the same note in succession when in the original melody such note repetition fell on a metrically weak beat. Such omission of note repetition made the melodic pause between one phrase and the next longer and thereby emphasised the phrase structure more markedly than did the original.

While Noel made more changes in the melodic than in the harmonic part of the music, the control pianist was quite unable to retain the harmony, and while his melody remained just about recognisable, his left hand played either nothing or completely wrong chords. In the next chapter we will hear of a study about the disassembling of chords by musically naïve children with autism. They were better able to do that than normal children, and we related this to the ability of those with autism to segment whole configurations. A chord is a very compelling and cohesive whole. Therefore the inability of the control pianist to identify and retain its constituents, and Noel's effortless success in doing so, supports the suggestion that a cognitive style of focusing on local elements may play a part in the development of some domain-specific high-level savant abilities. The control pianist told us that he found himself quite unable to listen, analyse and remember the melodic and harmonic parts simultaneously. He could simply not remember the chords at all. Noel on the other hand could identify and retain almost all their musical components.

Another striking aspect of Noel's playing was that he replaced given rhythmical configurations with others that occurred in their surrounding area. For these replacements he played notes that formed a sequence that was similar to the following one and to which he then supplied his own chords. This is just the kind of elaboration a proficient improviser might make. Thus Noel's improvisation, as well as his rare errors, were structure preserving, though elaborative.

Of course, I do not suggest that Noel's musical memory is comparable to that of some truly great musicians. Nevertheless, I am tempted to relate here an anecdote about Mozart who, when a youngster, was taken by his father to the Sistine Chapel in Rome to hear Allegri's choral piece *Miserere*. The score of this was kept under lock and key by the Vatican in order to induce pilgrims to come to Rome to hear it. It is recounted that after listening to this music, Mozart went back to the inn where he and his father were staying and there wrote out the full score of the piece with all of its many voices. The next day he put what he had written under his cap and smuggled it back into the chapel to listen again and check its accuracy. To his delight he found that he had only made very few errors, and thought that some of these would have fitted better into the piece than the original notes.

The second piece of music that the pianists heard and were asked to replay was a part of Bartok's *Mikrokosmos*. This was composed between 1926 and 1937 after the twelve-note scale had been introduced by Schönberg in 1923. He invented, or as he said he 'found', this system to avoid the new music falling into chaos. Unlike diatonic scales, the twelve-note scale progresses entirely in half-tone steps. Since the relationships between adjacent notes are all identical, there is no keynote. Consequently music based on this scale (atonal music) contains unfamiliar harmonic and melodic progressions, quite unlike those found in traditional Western music.

Bartok's piece played in this study is only mildly atonal. It is based on a whole-tone scale, contains intervals all of equal size (this time all whole tones instead of half tones). But the result is again music that has no obvious keynote and an unfamiliar harmonic and melodic landscape.

Like the piece by Grieg, the Bartok composition is developed through the repetition of elements taken from the first few bars. It is much shorter than 'Melody' and only two notes are ever simultaneously sounded. The music was first played through and then heard and played back in sections in the same manner as has been used with Grieg's composition. After this each participant was asked to play the piece from beginning to end.

When analysing the memory performance of Bartok's music, we found that the two pianists' respective ability to play this piece resulted in a changed pattern from that of playing Grieg's 'Melody'. As previously with the Grieg piece, the savant attempted to play more than the control pianist – 277 notes as compared with only 153. But 63 per cent of Noel's notes were wrong while the comparison musician made such mistakes in only 14 per cent of his rendering. The main feature of the savant's errors was the frequency with which notes were interchanged. The respective up or down pitch contour of the original was preserved, but the interval relations of one note to the next were destroyed. He also transposed left- and right-hand notes, though he sometimes corrected these slips. In contrast, at the final session the professional pianist played the whole piece almost faultlessly.

From these results it appears as if Noel had been trying to repeat Bartok's music like something which he had heard in a foreign musical language. Though he could remember some of the musical 'vocabulary items' (i.e. the separate notes that occurred), he did not understand the 'syntax' of this music (i.e. the notes' relationship to each other). This was in stark contrast to his replaying Grieg's tonal music. There, his familiarity with the music's structural characteristics and his ability to identify its melodic as well as harmonic components had been evident. Thus the few mistakes he made in replaying 'Melody' had been structure preserving and often took the form of appropriate improvisations. Such a restriction to their own native musical language is not found in all savant musicians. Some, as will be seen further on, might be described as being 'musically bilingual'. But here it was only within the context of his familiar musical idiom that Noel demonstrated his intuitive grasp of musical structures. The kind of difficulty he had with the Bartok piece is reminiscent of the findings reported by Smith and Tsimpli with the linguist Christopher, who was much better able to master new vocabularies of foreign languages than their unfamiliar grammars (Chapter 5).

The next question we asked about the nature of musical ability of savants was whether they could generate music of their own, as well as being able to reproduce music they had heard. O'Connor and I together with Sara Lee, a professional musician, identified five musical savants all living in units for people with mental handicaps. They were males aged between 18 and 58 years with IQs ranging from 50 to 69. Three of them had been diagnosed as suffering from autism, and the other two clearly showed autistic characteristics in their behaviour, such as remoteness from other people, an insistence on fixed routines, a limited range of interest and obsessional repetitive behaviour. Three of these savant musicians played the piano, one the recorder and the fifth sang his own songs, accompanying himself on percussion. This last participant also provided his own texts to his songs. Here is one of them:

> 'Let us thank our Father for this lovely day
> For the frosty meadows where we love to play
> Thank you for the daisies glistening in the dew
> Thank you for the sunshine and skies so blue
> In the living treetops birds are very small
> Children let us thank our Father for them all.'

There were five musical tasks that the participants were asked to perform. For the first they had to provide their own continuation of a partly played, previously unknown tune. For the second task they were asked to invent and play (or sing) a musical phrase. Third, they had to improvise an accompaniment for a tune on its second hearing; and fourth, they had to invent a tune together with its accompaniment. Finally, they had to improvise by playing together with a group of jazz musicians. These attempts by the savants were compared with those of five normal 13-year-old schoolchildren, whom their teachers had judged as being very musical. Unlike the savants, they all had regular music lessons, two playing the piano, one the clarinet, one the organ and one the flute. All the music that the participants had played in response to these different requirements was recorded. The recordings were then rated by two independent music experts on a five-point scale which ranged from judgements of 'unable to comply with task requirements' up to 'high-level performance'. The ratings included criteria for inventiveness, timing, balance in terms of phrase lengths, and good melodic shape and structure.

It emerged from this procedure that the schoolchildren had attempted to comply with almost all of the five task requirements, but had obtained relatively low scores on most of them. Only one child scored 5 for tune continuation and 4 for inventing an accompaniment. In contrast, the savants were much more selective, but on the few tasks they tried to comply with, they all obtained high ratings of 4 and 5. Thus the normal children were more enterprising in attempting most of what was asked of them, but overall they performed rather poorly. The savants' attempts were more patchy, but whenever they did have a go their performances were of a rather high level. The conclusion from these results was that the ability of musical savants was not confined to an outstanding musical memory, but extended to the generation and invention of music.

The next experiment with a savant musician was carried out by O'Connor and myself together with Donald Treffert. The savant in this study, Leslie, was brought to Treffert's attention when he heard him play the piano; he regarded him as the most remarkable savant he had ever encountered. Leslie was born prematurely with retrolental fibroplasia and when six months old had to have both eyes removed, so that he became totally blind. In addition, Leslie also suffers from cerebral palsy, which led to trouble with walking and impaired manual dexterity. But although he had, for instance, difficulties in eating with knife and fork, his general manual clumsiness did not prevent him from playing the piano with great virtuosity, thus demonstrating an astonishing modularity of dexterity that was confined to his piano playing. It reminded me of a friend who was severely affected by stuttering. Yet she was an enthusiastic amateur actress, and never stuttered once when speaking her part on stage.

Leslie was in the care of a remarkable woman who had great expertise in dealing with handicapped children. When he was between two and three years old, she noted that he barely spoke but could sing. He was remote and distant with other people, very restless, and when five and a half years old would still only imitate words and phrases that he had heard but would not talk spontaneously. When he was tested at the age of seven, he had an IQ of 59, which is about equivalent to the mental capacity of a normal three and a half to four year old. But at the same time his musical ability had also become apparent. He was given access to a piano by his foster mother who could play many songs by ear, an ability which Leslie soon shared with her. By the age of nine he had also learned to play the chord organ, but still did not engage in spontaneous talk. When aged 12 he had developed a lovely singing voice and would listen to music for many hours.

When Leslie was 14 years old his foster mother was woken one night by hearing him play part of Tchaikovsky's Piano Concerto No. 1 almost faultlessly. Leslie had heard this piece played on television the previous evening. He began to acquire a wide repertoire of classical music after listening to it and gave his first public concert when he was 22 years old. When Treffert later on contacted us, he told us that Leslie was also improvising on the piano and so he, O'Connor and I decided on an investigation of his ability in this respect.

As in the musical memory study with Noel that I have described, we used Grieg's 'Melody' and Bartok's mildly atonic whole-tone scale composition from his *Mikrokosmos*. Another musician was the control pianist. He had a degree in music and is an accomplished composer and keyboard player. Here again, as far as we could ascertain, both pieces of music had hitherto been unknown to the participants. Each piece was played once only. After this the control musician was asked to improvise on what he had just heard, whereas Leslie was told to 'go on playing music that goes well with what you have just listened to'.

Having first played a few bars of Grieg's 'Melody' note perfect, Leslie produced 215 bars of improvisations, which he played with enormous enthusiasm and verve. The professional pianist played 95 bars. While improvising, Leslie repeated Grieg's theme seven times and the other musician in his much shorter improvisation did this three times. Taking account of the length of the participants' respective playing, they both used proportionally the same percentages of related keys. But while Grieg had retained the original tonal centre of A minor and A major in 39 per cent of his composition, this was increased to 78 per cent by the control pianist, but reduced by Leslie to 18 per cent. While Grieg had not used any remote keys from the central one at all, and the control did this only very sparingly, Leslie played in remote keys for 13 per cent of the time. The professional musician also rarely used transitions (i.e. abrupt modulation from one key to another) and he played only one cadenza. In contrast, Leslie used both of these devices abundantly. Overall, the savant replaced Grieg's rather thin texture with something much more dense and though he never lost sight of the main theme and returned to it often, he interspersed this with extravagant flamboyant expansions. In contrast to Leslie's embellishments of Grieg's spare texture, the professional musician tended to retain it, and his improvisations were simple, reflective and restrained, as indeed is Grieg's own composition. But both participants demonstrated a high degree of musical understanding and their respective constraint or lack of it when improvising should be taken to have reflected their individual musical style and preference.

Turning to the improvisations following Bartok's mildly atonal composition, this music does not really allow for the kind of expansion that would encompass individual variations of style and yet remain within the musical idiom of the piece. Both pianists played their improvisations in the whole-tone scale for almost all the time. Leslie did this for 87 per cent and the control for 89 per cent. In the few changes that were made, both used half-tone and one and a half tone intervals rather than remaining in the whole-tone scale. Bartok's timing was maintained in most of the playing by the control and for more than half the time by Leslie. Time changes by both pianists mainly took the form of switching from the original 2/4 to the 3/4 beat. Overall, in improvising on Bartok's music the two participants resembled each other much more closely than they had done in their improvisations on the piece by Grieg, although for the Bartok, too, Leslie also gave a much richer interpretation, mostly by putting in more chords.

Leon Miller, whose research has broken new ground, has reported in his book *Musical Savants* that he repeated our studies with very similar results. For his child savant Eddie, whole-tone music clearly provided a novel and interesting challenge, but eventually the Bartok piece became part of his repertoire. However his assimilation to the whole-tone idiom was somewhat halting, whereas this was not the case with Grieg's 'Melody'. Another savant musician whom Miller tested responded enthusiastically to the Bartok piece, but filled it with so many chord embellishments that is was impossible to analyse. On the other hand he rendered Grieg's 'Melody' much more faithfully. Miller points out that as savants may well be less frequently exposed to whole-tone music, it is difficult to determine the extent to which preference or familiarity are involved in their rendering of it.

From our studies it seems that, in contrast to Noel, Leslie could be regarded as being musically bilingual. However, I have to qualify this conclusion, as in the last four bars of his Bartok improvisations Leslie seemed to have had enough of this idiom. He gave up this mode altogether, and in the final four bars of his playing instead reverted triumphantly and with great relish to the F major key and ended by playing repeatedly basic harmonic chords. The great conductor Bruno Walter had once written that it would be a hopeless experiment to withhold such a definite ending, and that it is the harmonic reconciliation that provides the feeling of elation and bliss which music provides. It seems that Leslie may have intuitively followed Bruno Walter's advice.

Arnold Schönberg, who had introduced his twelve-note system in 1923, maintained, as Picasso had done in regard to his new painting style, that he had not 'invented' this new musical system, but instead that he had 'found' it. However, it is quite clear that he had consciously set out to impose a new order on total atonality, which he feared would otherwise have led into chaos. Thus there can be no doubt that Schönberg's musical system, which became hugely influential, was a consciously pursued great intellectual endeavour, and the same applies to whole-tone music. It is perhaps all the more astonishing that in some of Schönberg's very late compositions he returned to the diatonic tonal idiom. Perhaps he had by then appreciated a somewhat similar though only partial truth stated much later in time, and in a different context, by the rock musician Jimi Hendrix: 'A musician, if he is a messenger, is like a child who has not been handled too many times by men, had not had too many fingerprints across his brain.' Perhaps it might not be too far-fetched to regard Noel and Leslie as just such messengers?

13

Autism and Savant Ability Revisited

Early on in this report I had stated a hypothesis, that if confirmed might help to explain why the majority of savants are autistic. Linda Pring and I had proposed that their cognitive style of focusing on separate elements and features of information might serve to provide autistic savants with the building blocks from which calendrical, musical, linguistic, numerical and pictorial structures would be gradually built up and extracted. But as savant ability often tends to emerge suddenly and spontaneously, it is difficult to identify the possible precursors that will lead to the manifestation of these gifts. I will therefore begin this chapter by reporting some preliminary indicators from studies with a group of autistic children without any obvious specific talents, who were compared with another group of intelligence-matched, non-autistic participants. We selected music as the domain for this investigation. Music seemed a suitable area for such a project, as children who suffer from autism or Asperger Syndrome generally like to listen to it. As far as I am aware, this series of studies is at present unique in attempting to connect directly some aspects of autistic cognition with savant ability. The experiments were carried out by Pamela Heaton while she was working with Linda Pring and myself, and concern the understanding of music by autistic children who have no special abilities within the musical domain.

Parents' reports, as well as clinical observations, indicate that many children with autism like and respond well to music. Often they prefer music to language and will sometimes follow requests when they are sung rather than spoken. Some children with autism who appear to be virtually mute may nevertheless sing words or musical phrases after very few hearings. Others listen to music for long periods, so this seems to be an idiom to which those with autism take readily and spontaneously. However, liking music does not necessarily imply its understanding. In addition to the emotional and aesthetic experiences it offers, musical understanding requires appreciation of the various structural aspects that it encompasses. Only a limited number of music's structural components will be considered here and these were selected in order to test the hypothesis that an autistic tendency towards segmented information processing might act as one possible precursor for the development of savant musical ability. The capacity to relate such single elements of music to each other was also investigated.

The first of this series of studies by Heaton, who is a trained musician as well as a psychologist, focused on absolute-pitch ability. This is defined here as a skill in identifying and labelling specific notes without reference to an external standard. Leon Miller has pointed out that all musical savants described in the literature have possessed absolute pitch, although it is found only rarely in normal populations, including professional musicians. However, as all musical savants have absolute-pitch ability, Miller has suggested that for them this may provide the building blocks for the implicit understanding of higher level musical structures. Thus although absolute pitch is not in itself sufficient for the manifestation of savant musical ability, it could nevertheless be a necessary precursor to it.

Ten boys with autism participated in this absolute pitch study. They were all attending a school for able autistic children and most, though not all, had approximately average levels of non-verbal intelligence. But all showed marked autistic features in their general behaviour which made it necessary for them to attend a special school. These autistic children were individually matched for level of mental development and intelligence with ten normal children. The participants were tested for their ability to identify and remember single differently pitched notes, and as a control condition identification and memory of word fragments was included. As the children were not familiar with note names, each note or speech sound was paired with a picture of an animal, whose name served as a label. When a child first heard a note or speech fragment, the experimenter pointed to one of the pictures saying 'this is the note the snake likes best' (or 'this is the note the fish/cat/bird likes best'). For the speech sounds the corresponding pictures were pig, duck, dog and cow. The procedure was repeated several times with each of the note/picture and speech sound/picture pairs. After this, the notes or speech sounds were each heard in random sequences, and the child was asked to identify the animal that liked this note or word fragment best. Identification was first tested two and a half minutes after following the familiarisation of notes or speech pairings with animal pictures, and again after a week's interval, when the familiarisation training was omitted.

When the results from this study of absolute pitch were subjected to a statistical analysis, it was found that there was no difference between the groups in either their initial identification or their memory for identifying the picture labels with speech sounds. However, when notes had to be identified and remembered, those with autism did significantly better than the control participants. In fact, they could identify more labelled musical notes after seven days than the controls could after two and a half minutes. Furthermore, four autistic participants achieved 100 per cent correct responses, while no normal child equalled such a performance.

These results indicate that musically naïve autistic children show superior pitch identification ability, and this nicely links their musical cognition with Miller's observation regarding the universality of absolute pitch among musical savants. In the present study the children had no special musical ability, yet the bias generally shown by those with autism to focus on single segments seemed to have led to superior pitch identification and memory. Thus the findings from the study go some way towards accounting for the predominance of those with autism among savants, although it remains to be established whether the ability to acquire such initial building blocks applies only to the musical domain or has wider implications. Further studies by Pamela Heaton confirmed the normal, or indeed the superior, musical skills of those with autism and I will briefly mention some of these experiments. The participants who took part in the studies I am going to describe were those who took part in the pitch experiment.

In one of these investigations the children were asked to disassemble chords. The chords used in this study were tonic triads, which comprise the first, third and fifth notes of the scale. Such chords are highly coalescing, as the third and fifth notes are represented in the overtones of the note that forms the root of the chord. But in view of the ability of those with autism to segment coherent configurations, for example block designs, it was predicted that they might also be better able than the controls to disassemble chords into their component tones.

This time the children were shown four new pictures of different animals. They were again told that each of these animals had a favourite note. Then each of four notes was sounded and they were told 'this is the camel's favourite note', etc. After going through this procedure several times with appropriate note/animal pairings, chords containing only three of the previously heard four notes were played. Before this, the children were told: 'You will now hear three of the four animal notes together, but this time the favourite note of one of the animals will be left out. Can you show me which animal's note is missing?' This was a difficult task, as it not only required the children to identify the three notes contained in the chord, but also to remember the one note that the chord did not contain. Nevertheless, the children with autism gave more correct responses than the control children whose performance was at chance level. The group difference proved statistically significant, thereby extending the conclusions drawn from the absolute-pitch study, that children with autism could not only identify and label single notes, but could also segment a musically coalescent note configuration. In addition, the identification of the missing note demonstrated a stable memory representation of all the chord's components. In this context the reader may recall the ability shown by the musical savant Noel to reproduce the harmonic accompaniment of Grieg's 'Melody'. In order to do this Noel had obviously identified the single components of the chords while the professional pianist seemed to have lacked this ability.

As has been pointed out, in order to recognise structural features it is not sufficient to identify and retain single separate components. In order to find our way without a map, we not only have to remember the separate street names that we encountered on a previous occasion of walking or driving to a place, but also have to know how the streets are interconnected and whether we have to turn right or left at a corner into another street. Musical pitch intervals are defined by the distance between two simultaneously or sequentially presented tones. Sequentially presented pitch intervals can go up or down, which means that the second note can be of a higher or lower frequency than the first.

In the next experiment, it was investigated how well such directional movements could be judged with variously sized pitch intervals. Thus it was asked whether children with autism had not only a better than average ability to identify and remember single pitches and segment chords into their constituent notes, but whether they could also relate notes to each other. Here, they had to decide whether small, medium or large pitch intervals had moved upwards or downwards. To make the task clear, the children were shown pictures of people ascending or descending a flight of stairs, and were told that notes could also go up or down. This was demonstrated by playing pairs of notes, in which the second one was higher or lower than the first, and it was explained that higher meant 'up' and lower meant 'down'. After such repeated demonstrations, 48 pairs of notes were played, the pitch differences between pair members ranging from one semitone to a whole octave. Half the intervals were descending and half were ascending, and there were sixteen of each small, medium and large interval types. The children had to point at the picture that showed the man going up or down the stairs to indicate the direction of the pitch interval.

The analysis showed a very different pattern of performance for the two groups. The comparison children could easily make correct judgements about medium and large pitch intervals, but they performed significantly worse with small pitch intervals. In contrast, the children with autism had no difficulty in judging these small intervals and showed overall high-level performances with all interval types.

For detecting the direction of pitch intervals between two sequentially presented notes, one needs not only to identify and remember them, but also to make a relational judgement about whether a second note is higher or lower than the first. That children with autism were better able than the controls to do this with notes which were only minimally different from each other suggests that they possess a high degree of acuity for this kind of information. Thus at least in this context, a superior ability by musically naïve children with autism to identify single pitches, to retain them in memory and to segment chords into their constituents, did not preclude an enhanced sensitivity in relating notes to each other. This goes beyond the superior local processing ability that is regarded as characteristic of those with autism. Therefore in the next study Heaton asked whether such an indicator towards musical coherence would also be evident in more complex musical configurations such as melodies.

Melodies provide multidimensional information including, for instance, such variables as tonality, rhythm and speed, with each of these components having quite firm definitions. However, despite this apparent complexity, nearly all of us can recognise a melody when we hear one and the aspects to which we are most sensitive are their general shapes, the rising and falling patterns of their overall contours. It has been shown that young children are especially sensitive to such musical contours and it is this aspect of a melody that is largely preserved in their singing. Thus melodies appear to be primarily perceived as coherent whole configurations, rather than consisting of a sequence of isolated elements. The question Heaton asked was whether autistic children, in contrast to controls, would perceive melodies in terms of their local constituents rather than as total musical patterns.

In the following study, 30 pairs of six-note melodies were played to the participants, who then had to judge whether the two melodies of a pair were the same or different. In ten pairs the two melodies were the same, and in the other two conditions they differed by only one note which occurred at different positions in the sequence. In ten pairs of these 'different' melodies, a note that had gone up in the first melody of the pair now went down in the second, thus violating the overall melody shape and harmonic structure. But in the second 'different' melody condition, the changed note differed only in pitch distance, but not in direction or harmonic structure. Thus here overall melodic shape and harmonic structure were preserved.

No differences between the autistic and normal children were found in this melody study. All participants detected differences between two melodies when the overall contour was violated, but tended to judge melodies in which the changed note maintained the contour as the same. Thus when processing melodies, single musical segments only became salient when they violated the overall melodic shape, and this was so not only for normal but also for autistic children. It was therefore concluded that, at least within the musical domain, children with autism were able to use contextual and global coherence as well as those without such a diagnosis.

Overall, the results obtained from these investigations of musical understanding by musically naïve children with autism showed that their tendency towards local processing and segmentation appears to convey an advantage, that allows them an enhanced identification of and discrimination between musical notes. But such a processing style did not entail an impaired ability to relate musical elements to each other. Even when, as in this melody experiment, the autistic participants had the option to process the melodies for detail, they instead responded to the music's global characteristics. What remains to be established is whether the musical understanding and a trend toward coherence which were demonstrated here are confined to the domain of music or whether they would also become apparent in other areas.

How then can the results obtained here with musically naïve autistic children help us to understand the savant phenomenon? Miller, in his outstanding book *Musical Savants*, has suggested that a route towards acquisition of savants' musical knowledge begins with their absolute-pitch ability. The identification and retention of individual notes provide the building blocks for a gradual development of an interconnected knowledge system about musical structures. The reader may recall that we had proposed a similar route towards calendar calculation ability. As with music, this begins with an interest in and memory for single items, in this instance isolated dates. The gradual extraction of connections between them eventually results in a knowledge base that mirrors calendar structure. Such structural knowledge will not only enable the savants to identify past day–date associations, or replay music they have heard, but also serves as a base for the generation of future dates or new music. Another example of such a route from parts to wholes is provided by Christopher's phenomenal facility for new vocabulary acquisitions (Chapter 5), though in this instance, as with Noel's musical memory, the mastering of new unfamiliar linguistic or musical 'grammars' appeared to be more difficult. But overall, within the domain where they are talented, autistic savants appear to use the strategy of taking a path from single units to a subsequent extraction of higher-order patterns and structures.

Until now, psychologists have not succeeded in analysing convincingly the component qualities that the concept of talent encompasses. But this does not entail the non-existence of inherent gifts that make use of whatever mental processes are available for their realisation. In his book *The Mind's Best Work*, D.N. Perkins has set out his criteria for defining the components of what he terms 'creativity' – the essence of talent and its realisation. The first and most central of these is that this is not a state of mind but an activity. It is about *making* or *doing* something. As I have repeatedly pointed out here, savants certainly fulfil this requirement. One example for this was that calendar calculators remembered calculated dates better than those they had merely studied. Another instance is that superior memory for visual detail was only evident in the drawings, rather then the mere observations of savant artists. Second, Perkins regards a plan or aim as essential, but it is doubtful whether this plays a prominent part in savant productions. However, Perkins qualifies such an overall planning requirement by proposing that rather than being always preoccupied with envisaging the finished work, new ideas may arise from the particulars of ongoing activity. This may indeed be how at least some savants proceed, and the way in which the savant artist Richard built up his pictures from layers of colour illustrates this strategy.

However, there is little indication in savants' artistic, musical or poetic productions that Perkins's requirements for continuous reassessing, re-doing and reorganising of creative output are in evidence. According to Gombrich, it may even be claimed that such self-criticism might be the most treasured heritage of Western art. An apparent absence of these processes in Kate's poetry led Adrian Pinkerton to observe that the poems read more like drafts than finished products. For her, as for savants in general, it is the activity that counts rather than the end result. Another requirement for true creative ability, which is certainly missing in savants, is a search for new forms of expression that characterise the history of Western art.

Of course, the mental impairments from which savants suffer set boundaries to the development of their talents. There are no savant geniuses about. None of them will discover a new mathematical theorem, or initiate a novel stylistic movement in the visual arts or in music. Neither will a savant pianist give a novel, revealing interpretation of a Beethoven piano sonata. Their mental limitations disallow and preclude an awareness of innovative developments in the areas of their special abilities. Their success will always have to be judged against the background of their general cognitive and affective restrictions. Nevertheless, their achievements are far above those to which most of us could aspire, and they deserve our respect and admiration.

As I had stated at the beginning of this research report, my aim has been to convey more than a sense of wonder about the puzzling phenomenon of savant ability. My main intention was to allow the reader an increased understanding of the mental strategies that seem to be employed by talented autistic individuals in order to make their given potentials realisable. I have done this through the qualitative analysis of individual achievements and by presenting the results that we have obtained in our group investigations. But collecting experimental data is of course never an end in itself. It merely serves as a basis from which conclusions about the mental processes that underlie the observed behaviour can be drawn. Such conclusions and interpretations in terms of theory are always open to revision. Unlike data derived from competently designed experiments, conclusions are always provisional. New results will accumulate that will supplement, contradict, revise, or much more rarely confirm, such conclusions and explanatory theories. This is the only way our knowledge can progress.

I hope that I have also been able to convey some of the intense pleasure that these research pursuits have given me. It is this enjoyment of 'doing it' that should motivate a new generation of experimental psychologists to attempt to prove me wrong in my conclusions about the nature of autistic savant talent. As Diderot, the eighteenth-century writer and philosopher, said: 'It can be required of me that I look for the truth, but not that I should find it.'

Further Reading

Frith, U. (1989) *Autism: Explaining the Enigma.* Oxford: Blackwell.

Frith, U. (1991) *Autism and Asperger's Syndrome.* Cambridge: Cambridge University Press.

Happé, F. (1994) *Autism: An Introduction to Psychological Theory.* London: UCL Press.

Hermelin, B. and O'Connor, N. (1970) *Psychological Experiments with Autistic Children.* Oxford: Pergamon Press.

Miller, L.K. (1989) *Musical Savants.* Mahwah, NJ: Lawrence Earlbaum.

Perkins, D. N. (1981) *The Minds Best Work.* Harvard, MA: Harvard University Press.

Rutter, M. and Schopler, E. (eds) (1978) *Autism: A Reappraisal of Concepts and Treatment.* London: Plenum Press.

Sacks, O. (1995) *An Anthropologist on Mars.* London: Picador.

Schopler, E. and Mesibov, G.B. (eds) (1983) *Learning and Cognition in Autism.* London: Plenum Press.

Schopler, E. and Mesibov, G.B. (1992) *High Functioning Individuals with Autism.* London: Plenum Press.

Smith, N. and Tsimpli, M. (1995) *The Mind of a Savant.* Oxford: Blackwell Publishers.

Treffert, A.D. (1989) *Extraordinary People.* London: Bantam.

Volksmar, F. (ed) (1999) *Autism and Pervasive Developmental Disorders.* Cambridge: Cambridge University Press.

Subject Index

Author Index

Some autistic people have singular talents of various sorts, existing in strange isolation from the rest of their minds. While such 'savant' talents have been described, anecdotally, for a century or more, Beate Hermelin has been a pioneer in their scientific investigation. In Bright Splinters of the Mind, *she brings together the results of her more than twenty years' research, and presents a highly original and systematic analysis of a range of autistic talents – artistic, musical, linguistic, mathematical – showing that while they might seem to be so odd and special, they provide essential clues to the nature of all intelligent thinking. This analysis is embedded in an engrossing narrative of Dr. Hermelin's own personal involvement and passion. This then is research which is rigorous, but has an intensely human face.* Bright Splinters of the Mind *is simply but beautifully written, and will, I think, fascinate and move a wide range of readers.*

– *Dr Oliver Sacks*